NICHOLAS H

THE
SCANDAL
OF
CHRISTIAN
DISUNION

Why it must STOP **immediately**

kevin mayhew

**kevin
mayhew**

First published in Great Britain in 2017 by Kevin Mayhew Ltd
Buxhall, Stowmarket, Suffolk IP14 3BW
Tel: +44 (0) 1449 737978 Fax: +44 (0) 1449 737834
E-mail: info@kevinmayhew.com

www.kevinmayhew.com

9 8 7 6 5 4 3 2 1 0

ISBN 978 1 84867 892 7
Catalogue No. 1501544

Cover design by Rob Mortonson
© Image used under licence from Shutterstock Inc.
Edited by Virginia Rounding
Typeset by Angela Selfe

Printed and bound in Great Britain

Contents

To my brother Jesuits of the South African Region,
with gratitude.

About the Author

Nicholas King SJ is a Jesuit Priest who taught for many years in South Africa, and then at Oxford University. After a sabbatical year as a Visiting Professor at the School of Theology and Ministry at Boston College, and another year as Academic Director of Theology at St Mary's University, Twickenham, he is now Lecturer in Biblical Studies at Heythrop College, University of London, and Provincial's Delegate for Formation for the British Jesuit Province.

In 2014 Kevin Mayhew published his translation of the entire Greek Bible; and in the same year Nicholas also produced *The Helplessness of God* (1501439), on how governance is done in the Bible.

Preface

Why write a book about the disunity of Christians? Is not that too depressing a topic? Is it not an insoluble problem, better left on one side? Well, perhaps; but this book has its origins in three converging factors. The first was the realisation, through my years of teaching, of how remarkably close were the links I discovered with other Christians. I had already experienced something of the sort in my work in South Africa, noting a change in relationship with dominies in the Dutch Reformed Church, as I learned more of the power of God's word, revealed in Scripture, and they came to appreciate more the incarnational and sacramental side of Catholicism, as well as giving expression to their yearning for something called 'spirituality'. For some reason, though, this sense of closeness was much more evident in my work at Oxford; it seemed to me that the Spirit was speaking in these warm and deepening relationships.

The second was an invitation by the Jesuit Institute of South Africa to give a series of lectures in their Winter School for 2015. Originally the plan was to do something on John's Gospel, but it was borne in on me that the question of the reunion of Christianity was a more urgent one. At a time when it was becoming clear that religion was a force that had to be taken seriously worldwide, and that Christianity, which has a good deal of wisdom to offer on the place of religion in the world, was suffering from a divided voice which prevented it from being heard, it seemed good to attempt another look at the question.

The third converging factor was the experience of teaching New Testament, and the language in which the New Testament was written, to students at Oxford University (and then, subsequently, at the School of Theology and Ministry at Boston College, and at St Mary's University, Twickenham) from all religious backgrounds and none, and hearing them respond with the discovery that, after all, this Christian Scripture had something to say to them. My students were atheist, agnostic, Hindu, Jewish, Buddhist, and members of all kinds of Christian denominations, and they read the texts with intelligence and with a sense that there was a dialogue to be had. More specifically, I started to realise that Christians could sensibly read the New Testament together and agree far more than they disagreed. It seemed to me that this was a helpful discovery, useful for the broken and darkened world in which we live.

The shape of this book is fairly simple. In the first chapter we shall look at the scandal of Christian disunion, and in particular at the mystery whereby perfectly good people seem content to live with the scandal. Then we shall look at each of the 27 documents that constitute the New Testament, in the following order:

Paul (because he came first), then the Johannine literature apart from Revelation (because these documents show an awareness of divisions), then Mark, Matthew, and Luke. After that, there will be a chapter on the Book of Revelation, where the temperature is fairly high, and finally the 'Catholic Epistles' (by which I mean anything not mentioned so far). The point here will be to demonstrate that each of our NT authors was well aware of the possibility of divisions in the Church (they are not, therefore, an invention of the sixteenth century), and that they had a way of coping with the divisions, what I shall term, perhaps a bit too naively (though it is in line with the leadership currently being given us by Pope Francis and other contemporary church leaders), 'keeping their eyes on God and on Jesus'. At the end of the book we shall look at one particular issue that apparently divides Christians of the Roman Catholic persuasion (to which I belong) from other Christians, namely the role given to Mary the mother of Jesus, and in particular to the two teachings about her Immaculate Conception and her Assumption, and whether the Catholic position represents an unbridgeable gap for Christians from other traditions.

It is important to say that there is nothing new about divisions in the Church, and all of us could tell stories of silly behaviour (you might like to give your own examples at this point) of Christians faced with interdenominational tensions. The fact remains that the Church has, especially today, an absolute duty to proclaim the gospel; but we always need to check that it is indeed the gospel that we are trying to preach. For we are fallible and sinful – and we can get it wrong.

One last thing to say is that when reading for this book I found far too much material; the more I read, the more I found. So in the course of these pages I shall be aiming to see the wood rather than the trees; to that end, the book has been kept deliberately short.

And a final note: Bible quotations are my own translation (although they may not necessarily coincide with what you will find in my published translation).

CHAPTER 1

The mystery of anti-ecumenism

Introduction

It may be worth at the outset saying just a word about the title of this book. In what sense is Christian disunion a 'scandal'? Some will argue that there have always been divisions in Christianity; others that disunity may not be 'a scandal – more a sign of growth',[1] and that we should not be afraid to have a clear position on matters where Christians do indeed hold different views. Truth and integrity are important values. That is true; and it may be that disagreement between Christians is a sign of adult honesty; in that sense it is not a scandal.[2] I want, however, to argue that it is a scandal at least in this sense – that in a world that desperately needs the gospel, those who are not Christian may resist its invitation solely on the grounds of the way they see Christians behaving towards each other, for example in the Church of the Holy Sepulchre in Jerusalem.

The mystery of anti-ecumenism

The scandal of Christian disunion gives rise to one of the profound mysteries of our time – that whereas everyone, or at least all the great and the good, are agreed on the importance of restoring the unity of the body of Christ, as soon as you get anywhere near it, suddenly there is a profound counter-reaction, sometimes angry, sometimes merely coldly indifferent. At several stages in the last half-century there has been in various quarters immense enthusiasm for the ecumenical project; but for a number of different reasons this has been succeeded by despair. So, for example, Bruno Delorme[3] was able to dismiss it as 'la grande illusion de ce siècle', and many people in the 1990s spoke of the 'ecumenical winter', while the distinguished Irish ecumenist Michael Hurley SJ wrote, sadly, of the slow dance of negotiations between the Catholic and the Orthodox Churches that '[b]etween East and West there is fixed a great chaos of

---

1. Such as my eminent colleague Dr Philip Endean SJ, in a private communication.
2. Jesus himself could evidently be quite divisive, of course. See, for example, Luke 12:49-53: 'I came to throw fire on the earth, and how I wish it were already kindled! I have a baptism to be baptised, and how I am in distress until it is completed! Do you think that I came to give *peace* on the land? No – I'm telling you, but *division*: for from now on there will be five in one household, divided three against two and two against three. They shall be divided father against son and son against father, mother against daughter and daughter against mother, mother-in-law against her daughter-in-law and daughter-in-law against mother-in-law.'
3. In *Lumière Et Vie* 45/5, December 1996, pp.75-80.

lovelessness and lack of trust'.[4] This chapter is an attempt to take stock of where we are in the journey, before asking whether there are any signs of hope. My suggestion is that there is an invitation here to engage in our vocation to love; and as Jesus experienced, along with many of those who have given themselves to the difficult business of loving, not everyone reacts in joy to that invitation, and there will always be those (and there will always be a part of each of us) who respond with precisely cold indifference or anger.

Resisting the beguilement of easy solutions

There are two seductions that we have to avoid here. The first is that of playing what you might call the 'blame game'; the second is that of focusing on particular individuals. The blame game, roughly speaking, is that of determining whose fault is the division of the body of Christ; so Catholics, for example, might be inclined to point the finger at the Reform movement in Christianity, and say, 'It was you who abandoned the Church that Christ founded,' while Calvinists might share the view of the gifted theologian from whom they take their name that 'it was Rome (because of its essential corruption of word and sacrament) which had seceded and largely unchurched itself'.[5] The other seduction is that of singling out for blame or praise this person or that: Pope Francis, for example, or the late Reverend Ian Paisley. For all human beings are of their time, and need to be seen and heard in their context; the important thing is that we should pay attention to what is really going on. The task for us is not so much to concentrate on one religious leader rather than another, as to listen out for what the Spirit is saying in particular people. So what we have to do is to discern: and if in this particular person's attitudes and actions we find an agreeable warmth, or in what that other person says or does there is a repellent sense of winter, that may be a sign of where God is leading us.

So the aim of this chapter is to try to clear a way through the jungle, and peer hopefully for a way ahead. Since it often seems to be the case that both Catholics and non-Catholics (not to mention persons of no religious belief whatever) are inclined to blame Roman authorities for any ecumenical difficulties, I propose to look first at what has been said by recent Popes, to make it clear that it is illegitimate, for faithful Catholics for example, to resist the ecumenical imperative on the grounds that ecumenism is a betrayal of our religious history. The Popes of the last half-century are unanimous in summoning us to rebuild the body of Christ; and not since Pius XI in 1928 has a Pope given expression

---

4. Michael Hurley SJ, *Christian Unity: An Ecumenical Second Spring?* (Veritas, 1998), p.40. It is possible that he meant to write 'chasm' rather than 'chaos', a reference to Luke 16:26, but either word will do.
5. Calvin, *Institutes*, IV, 2, referred to in Hurley, *Christian Unity*, p.156.

to the view that ecumenism is a matter of all Christians returning to the Roman fold.[6] In subsequent sections, I shall look at some of the obstacles to ecumenical activity, some hopeful signs that suggest a possible way ahead, and, finally the absolute requirement today that Christians (and other believers in God, but that is another long story) should work together in the face of the needs of our world. Finally, it seems important to say that the overarching theme of this book is the challenging invitation to living out the quadriliteral word 'love', despite the anger and rejection that love often encounters.

Recent Popes on the ecumenical movement

For all sorts of reasons, Pope John XXIII is a good place at which to start. Fifty years ago he appeared, to everyone's surprise, in the Vatican, with that beaming smile, which now, under Pope Francis, is being seen once more in that place where (for a variety of reasons) a smile has not always been the order of the day, and with his profound, but from certain points of view quite threatening, insight that 'what unites us is much greater than what divides us'.[7] He made it clear that the 'compelling motive' for his calling of the Second Vatican Council, which we are now slowly beginning to live out, was the unity of the Church: 'The Catholic Church . . . considers it her duty to work actively so that there may be fulfilled the great mystery of that unity which Jesus Christ invoked with fervent prayer from his heavenly Father on the eve of his sacrifice.'[8]

His successor, Paul VI, had already in the first session of the council, while he was still Cardinal Montini, Archbishop of Milan, spoken significantly of 'the inadequacy of the current understanding of the Church as a visible society founded by Christ; it was rather Christ himself using human beings as instruments to bring salvation to all mankind';[9] he made it clear that he saw dialogue as 'an exchange of gifts'. This is a really revolutionary notion, involving the ideas that, first, the Catholic Church is not, after all, a perfect society, and, second, that other Christians have something to bring to the table from which we are in a position to learn. Once he became Pope, Montini continued with this line; dealing with the readiness of many Christian theologians to accept a

---

6. Mortalium animos, 1928, available at http://w2.vatican.va/content/pius-xi/en/encyclicals/documents/hf_p-xi_enc_19280106_mortalium-animos.html: 'the union of Christians can only be promoted by promoting the return to the one true Church of Christ of those who are separated from it, for in the past they have unhappily left it'. Paragraph 10. And for Pius XII, compare Mystici Corporis: http://w2.vatican.va/content/pius-xii/en/encyclicals/documents/hf_p-xii_enc_29061943_mystici-corporis-christi.html, with its emphasis on the necessarily 'visible' nature of the body of Christ. We should also notice the Pope's strict condemnation of anything that compels a person 'to embrace the Catholic faith against his will' (para 104). Strictly speaking, *Mystici Corporis* does not address the question of the ecumenical movement; and in any event it needs to be seen against the background of Pius XII's horror at the war which engulfed Europe at that time (June 1943), with Catholics fighting on all sides, to which he clearly hoped that the Church would provide an answer.

7. Quoted at vatican2voice.org/6unity/restore_unity.htm

8. *Ad Petri Cathedram* §42-44, 1959.

9. Edward Yarnold SJ, *They are in Earnest: Christian Unity in the Statements of Paul VI, John Paul I, John Paul II* (St Paul Publications, 1982), p.3.

papacy conceived as a universal primacy, he commented on one of the difficulties implicit in this idea, when he insisted that the office of the Pope is 'not a supreme authority puffed up with spiritual pride, but a primacy of service, a ministration of love'. [10] And he warned the Secretariat for Christian Unity that 'the Pope, as we well know, is undoubtedly the gravest obstacle in the path of ecumenism'.[11] Admitting that difficulty, and tackling its implications, is a challenge for our day, one to which Pope Francis is instinctively responding, and so finding a response from others who do not share his Catholic faith.

Nor did it come to an end with the death of Pope Paul, only to resurface under the present Pontiff. Pope John Paul II, often regarded as instinctively conservative, insisted, in his important encyclical *Ut Unum Sint*, that 'ecumenism, the movement promoting Christian unity, is not just some sort of "appendix" which is added to the Church's traditional activity. Rather, ecumenism is an organic part of her life and work, and consequently must pervade all that she is and does.'[12] So loyal Catholics have no choice but to work for Christian unity: 'it must be like the fruit borne by a healthy and flourishing tree which grows to its full stature'.[13] Nor is the Pope afraid to recognise that the holder of his office may himself be an obstacle, and that he 'must fervently make his own Christ's prayer for that conversion which is indispensable for "Peter" to be able to serve his brethren'.[14] Once again, here we have a Bishop of Rome drawing attention to the ecumenical difficulties that he may pose to other Christians.

His successor, Pope Benedict XVI, occasionally did and said things that might suggest a different direction from that of his immediate predecessors; but, careful theologian that he was, he insisted, on the very day after his election, in an address to the cardinals who had elected him, that the fostering of the unity of Christians would lie at the very heart of his ministry, and went on to say: 'Peter's current Successor takes on as his primary task the duty to work tirelessly to rebuild the full and visible unity of all Christ's followers. This is his ambition, his impelling duty. He is aware that good intentions do not suffice for this. Concrete gestures that enter hearts and stir consciences are essential, inspiring in everyone that inner conversion that is the prerequisite for all ecumenical progress.'[15] One important element that Benedict brings to the question is the absolute importance of Jesus; and it will be the argument of this book that, for Christians to find an answer to

---

10. *Ecclesiam Suam*, 1964; see Yarnold, *They are in Earnest*, p.26.
11. 28 April 1967; see Yarnold, *They are in Earnest*, p.66.
12. 25 May 1995; see: 'UT UNUM SINT: On commitment to Ecumenism', available at: http://w2.vatican.va/content/ john-paul-ii/en/encyclicals/documents/hf_jp-ii_enc_25051995_ut-unum-sint.html (accessed 9 December 2016).
13. Ibid.
14. Ibid.
15. See the interesting article by Fr Ronald Roberson on the North American Bishops' website: 'Pope Benedict XVI and Ecumenism: A Retrospective', available at: http://www.usccb.org/beliefs-and-teachings/ecumenical-and-interreligious/ pope-benedict-xvi-and-ecumenism-a-retrospective.cfm (accessed 9 December 2016).

the scandal of our disunion, it will be essential for us to look first and foremost at Jesus. So Pope Benedict told the bishops of the United States that:

> Confronted with these deeper questions[16] concerning the origin and destiny of mankind, Christianity proposes Jesus of Nazareth. He, we believe, is the eternal *Logos* who became flesh in order to reconcile man to God and reveal the underlying reason of all things. It is he whom we bring to the forum of inter-religious dialogue.

The ardent desire to follow in his footsteps spurs Christians to open their minds and hearts in dialogue. For those who may be nervous on the ecumenical journey, the Pope offers some reassurance: 'We have no reason to fear, for the truth unveils for us the essential relationship between the world and God.' There is the indispensable basis of our confidence in the ecumenical journey of love.

And what of Pope Francis, the incumbent of the See of Peter at the time of writing? He is not a 'careful theologian' in the sense that is true of his immediate predecessor; but he has a sure instinct, and what he does is to radiate an effusion of love, in symbolic actions, and rather striking utterances, which do not appear to be calculated on the basis of 'how it will play', as a public relations consultant might advise, but simply speak 'from the heart'. To take an example virtually at random, this is how his visit to Turkey, a country where religious divisions have immensely serious implications, was described: 'Francis, bowing to receive a kiss and blessing from the head of the Eastern Orthodox Church on himself and the Church of Rome during a prayer service in Istanbul on Saturday, gave physical expression to the longing for full unity between the ancient Churches.'[17] That powerful and simple gesture says it all; and Bartholomew, the Orthodox Patriarch of Constantinople, made the key point, shared by all responsible Christians that 'the Church exists not for itself, but for the world and humanity'. Earlier that year the Pope had taken the bold step of visiting a Pentecostal church in Italy, which provoked the Italian Evangelical Alliance into a statement that criticised Catholic teaching as incompatible with Scripture, and warning Pentecostal and evangelical communities not to go down that road.[18] Francis is not, however, in the game of winning friends; he was well aware, as he made clear, that he would be attacked for taking that step. He is playing a far deeper game than merely being nice to people. It is rather that he looks at the world as it is, with all its agonising problems, and recognises the need for

---

16. Questions such as the origin and destiny of humankind, the nature of good and evil, as a necessary prolegomenon to helping solve the problems of the world. This speech, delivered on 17 April, 2008, can be found at http://www.vatican.va/holy_father/benedict_xvi/speeches/2008/april/documents/hf_ben-xvi_spe_20080417_other-religions_en.html
17. In *The Tablet*, 6 December 2014, pp.4-5.
18. Reported in http://www.catholicnews.com/data/stories/cns/1403141.htm

Christians to journey together towards the Lord.[19] And it is Francis who has astonished the world by saying the following about the disunity of Christians:

- 'Who is at fault? All of us are. We are all sinners. There is only one who is right, and that is our Lord.'

- 'Our divisions must not be accepted with resignation.'

- 'If Christians ignore the Lord's call to unity, they risk ignoring the Lord himself and the salvation he offers.'

- 'Our divisions represent a major obstacle to our witness to the gospel in the world.'

- 'Unity comes about in journeying.'[20]

Francis is here coming back to a theme that he had already played in his well-received apostolic exhortation, *Evangelii Gaudium*,[21] where he insists on the importance of 'sincere trust in our fellow pilgrims, putting aside all suspicion or mistrust, and turn[ing] our gaze to what we are all seeking: the radiant peace of God's face'. Here there is none of the careful theological language of his predecessor, or of Cardinal Walter Kaspar whom we shall shortly be considering, but a going straight to the heart of the matter, in language that ordinary people can understand. There is more to it than mere vulgarisation, however: Francis sees a desperate urgency, given the state of our world. 'The immense numbers of people who have not received the gospel of Jesus Christ cannot leave us indifferent.' We should be clear that this sentiment does not spring from a sense that it would be nice to have a few more Christians in our churches; it is, rather, that there are people who are suffering because of our differences: 'Signs of division between Christians in countries ravaged by violence add further causes of conflict on the part of those who should instead be a leaven of peace.' Then he alludes to the words of John XXIII, to which we referred earlier, when he writes 'How many important things unite us!', and to Paul VI in *Ecclesiam Suam*, when, using an example of dialogue with the Orthodox, he argues that 'we Catholics have the opportunity to learn more about the meaning of episcopal collegiality and their experience of synodality', and concludes, echoing Paul VI: 'Through an exchange of gifts, the Spirit can lead us ever more fully into truth and goodness.'[22]

---

19. And compare his very touching address to Lutherans on 21 October, 2013, reported at http://www.catholic.org/news/international/europe/story.php?id=52824
20. 'Unity is a journey, not a destination, says the Pope to the Pontifical Council for Promoting Christian Unity, 10.11.2016', Holy See Press Office. Available at https://press.vatican.va/content/salastampa/en/bollettino/pubblico/2016/11/10/161110a.html (accessed 9 December 2016).
21. Available in English translation: *Evangelii Gaudium – the joy of the Gospel* (CTS, 2013).
22. *Evangelii Gaudium*, p.117.

Then there is Cardinal Kasper himself; I mention him here, not because he is likely to be elected Pope, but rather because he is saying the kinds of things that animate the present Pope, and which excite a good deal of opposition, but point in a direction that extends the teaching that we have cited from John XXIII, Paul VI, John Paul II and Benedict XVI. The last-named made this striking statement during the Week of Prayer for Christian Unity 2012, just before he resigned:

> The full and visible Christian unity that we long for demands that we let ourselves be transformed and that we conform ourselves ever more perfectly to the image of Christ. The unity we pray for requires an inner conversion that is both common and personal. It is not merely a matter of cordiality or cooperation, it is necessary above all to strengthen our faith in God, in the God of Jesus Christ, who spoke to us and made himself one of us. It is necessary to enter into new life in Christ, who is our true and definitive victory; it is necessary to open ourselves to one another, understanding all the elements of unity that God keeps for us and gives us ever anew.[23]

Now Cardinal Kasper and the erstwhile Cardinal Ratzinger often found themselves in disagreement on matters theological, and their style was very different; but here they run quite close together. For Kasper has recently published an important book on the Church,[24] indicating how we might look ahead. At the heart of the matter is the ecumenical perception that Christ's Church is rooted in the Christ event, not 'merely in a concept nor in a privileged historical period, but in a living, organic reality'.[25] Kasper is part of a long-standing German tradition that sees the Spirit as dynamic, leading the Church forward into the fullness of truth; so that those of us who cry 'halt', fearful that we may be abandoning hard-won doctrinal insights, may in fact be unfaithful to the Spirit. Kasper expresses it in this way, which may be helpful for our ecumenical journey:

> The Church is much more of a dialectical double-movement in relationship with its 'origin in fullness'. *Retrospectively*, it must always take as its norm the truth revealed once and for all: it needs constant renewal from its origin, especially constant renewal from the witness of Scripture. At the same time, the Church must *prospectively* enter into each new situation and pay attention to the 'signs of the time'. In this double-movement, the Spirit leads in ever-new ways into the fullness of truth.

---

23. https://w2.vatican.va/content/benedict-xvi/en/.../hf_ben-xvi_aud_20120118.html. (18 January 2012). Log-in details required.
24. *Katholische Kirche: Wesen, Wirklichkeit, Sendung* (Herder, 2011). This has now been translated into English.
25. See John R. Sachs SJ, *Catholicism in a New Key*, in *The Theology of Cardinal Walter Kasper*, eds. Kristin M. Colberg and Robert A. Krieg (Liturgical Press, 2014), pp.170-188, a very helpful article which sets Kasper in his context, and from which much of the next few paragraphs is taken. This citation is found at p.171.

For Kasper, 'the ecumenical movement towards true Christian unity will enable each of the churches and Christian communities to discover elements of the Christian life that had been dormant or inadequate and then to incorporate these elements in new forms into its Christian life'.[26] The Church is always on a journey forward in love, whose final shape cannot, from where we stand, be determined. Here Kasper stands very close to where Pope Francis finds himself; and the two of them may well be an important signpost on our ecumenical journey, which is always heading, Spirit-led, into the future, and not towards the restoration of an all too often illusory past.

Obstacles to the ecumenical dialogue

So, looking ahead, what does the journey before us look like? Our first task must be to recognise the obstacles in our way; and the only obstacles that we can do anything about are not those that we detect in others. The obstacles that you and I have to deal with are those within ourselves. And there are several of these, which give us grounds for examining our consciences. The first is an observation of mine, which I cannot demonstrate, and which you are therefore quite at liberty to reject; but it seems to me that *unless a person is really at ease in their own religious tradition it is very hard to engage in negotiation with those from other religions or other Christian denominations*. My impression of those who are most impassioned against ecumenical dialogue is that they fear that the apple-cart may be completely upset if they allow the 'opposition' to have anything at all that they can teach us. In this context I noticed the observation of a senior Catholic prelate who, discreetly expressing his opposition to the Family Synod on which Pope Francis has put so much weight, suggested that this kind of decision-making was 'a bit Protestant', as though that observation would put an end to the Pope's manner of proceeding.

A second obstacle is connected with the first; it is the sense that we have nothing at all to learn from other Christians (never mind people of other religions or none – it is quite clear that the Pope thinks that all our brothers and sisters in the human race have something to tell us that is from God). Whenever Christians find themselves thinking (and we have all done this) that 'I know it all', then we should watch out. The Syro-Phoenician woman in Mark's Gospel makes Jesus change his mind, and recognise that he did not, after all, 'know it all' (Mark 7:24-30). She was not only a foreigner but also a woman and a member of another religion, never mind another denomination.

The third obstacle is that of unbendingly clinging to ancient insights, the more determinedly because those insights were hard-won. We can all think of

---

26. Ibid., p.178.

beliefs in our ancestral traditions for which our ancestors doggedly and loyally fought, and it is very proper to admire those ancestors for their courage. We may, however, have to recognise that in another age those beliefs have to be differently expressed. You will be able to think of instances in the life of Jesus where he challenged ancestral traditions, but you might instead like to reflect on what Jeremiah did, probably at a time when it would have seemed like grave disloyalty to the national religious project, when he warned his fellow Israelites: 'Don't put your trust in illusions, saying "These are the Temple of YHWH, the Temple of YHWH, the Temple of YHWH"' (Jeremiah 7:4). As the enemy massed at the gates, this was not what the people wanted to hear about their central religious symbol, and it must have seemed a terrible betrayal. But Jeremiah was right.

A fourth obstacle is the opposite one, that of rushing ahead of the Spirit; the difficulty of a prophet is that he or she can see earlier than the rest of us where things are going, and may tend to go there too soon. It is not that they are wrong, more that the Spirit invites us to travel together. One example in our age of an insight that did not immediately appeal to all the Church would be the realisation of the inseparable link between gospel and social justice, or responsible care of our planet. For a biblical parallel you might think of Philip baptising the Ethiopian eunuch, after the most minimal catechesis (Acts 8:26-40).

Then, fifthly, there is what the ancients used to call *odium theologicum.* There is that in religious discourse that makes people rise up in condemnation of those who hold different views; and it has to be admitted that condemning other people is enormous fun and makes us feel so much better. But it is a tendency that we have to recognise in ourselves and eschew. It is the sort of reaction that Jesus aroused when he said to his compatriots and co-religionists at the festival of Sukkoth in Jerusalem that they were not listening to God; their response, remarkably insulting in the context, was: 'Aren't we right to say that you are a Samaritan and have a demon?' (John 8:48). We can each of us imagine a situation in which a similar remark might be trembling on our lips, and resolve, next time, to swallow it. It is much more fun, of course, to be able to blame others; at times it can feel as though our identity depends on others being wrong, and we need to be aware of that tendency of ours, and correct it.

A sixth obstacle to ecumenical progress is the refusal to ask what the Spirit might be saying to us. Our task is to be forever alert to the lightness of the Paraclete's invitation rather than cling to the heavy burden of our outdated certainties. That was what was going on when Paul and Barnabas were criticised for not compelling their Gentile male converts to undergo circumcision, which, their opponents could reasonably argue, was 'what the Bible says'. We have in Acts 15:1-35 a fairly diplomatic account of this controversy, while in Galatians Paul rather lets himself go on the subject (Galatians 2:1-14); for he had grasped the very new and shocking thing that the Spirit was saying to the Church, namely that the boundary-marker of circumcision was no longer applicable for non-Jews who came to Christ. This is something that we no longer think twice about, so obvious does it seem to us; but to our forebears in that first century it was an issue of immense significance, a controversy that could have torn the Jesus movement apart. What they did, and what we have to do, is listen to that powerful and insistent, if at times decidedly uncomfortable, voice, and do what we are bidden, which is to look out for the presence of Jesus, and to respond to the Father's call. Divisions are to be expected in the Church, and they tell us something important, but we have to work to overcome them. At all costs, we must beware a godless rigidity (the certainty that 'I know what the Church should be like'). And how are we to do that? By keeping our eyes on God, imitating Jesus, and by listening for the Holy Spirit.

We might do well to learn from our brothers and sisters who are Jews;[27] for them, engagement and argument is admissible, because they all know that they belong, because of upbringing and ancestry or where they come from. So they know that they cannot be expelled. Some[28] argue that for Christians it is all a matter of what you believe, even if the expression of it changes down the centuries. So it is that in Christianity, unlike Judaism, accusations of 'heresy' become common, and questions of orthodoxy become most important. History tells us that it is often quite a close call, whether or not a particular proposition turns out to be deemed heretical; and, of course, perceptions shift over the centuries. An eminent lawyer of my acquaintance speaks of the Catholic Church's over-emphasis on 'pelvic sins' (for example, the unconventional domestic arrangements of those who are otherwise exemplary loving Catholics). It is a good question to ask: why do we talk more about the excommunication of such people, and less about the inadmissibility to communion of those Catholics who:

- Foster anti-Semitism and enhance racial tension

- Knowingly exploit the world's resources

- Ignore the plight of the poor

- Persecute immigrants

- Under-pay their workers

---

27. In this context it is now of the greatest importance to read the book by Rabbi Jonathan Sachs, *Not in God's Name, Confronting Religious Violence* (London: Hodder & Stoughton), 2015.
28. I owe this insight to a remark made by Professor Amy-Jill Levine in a decidedly lively lecture at Boston College.

- Invest in nuclear weapons

- Betray Jesus, immediately after the Last Supper

- Adopt Arian or Docetic Christology?

All these obstacles, finally, can be summed up in one comprehensive failure, on the part of each of us, which is, quite simply, our lack of love. We feel 'better' if there are other people whom we can dismiss as 'wrong'. So we have a certain emotional investment in ourselves being always 'right'. There is no need for us to despair, for this is part of the human condition; but, make no mistake, that is what is going on here. We who care for the body of Christ should recite to ourselves, several times a day, the words of Augustine:[29] 'dilige et quod vis fac'.[30] That is the uncomfortable example that we are today being offered by Pope Francis. And love will be found to have the lightness that human beings look for, as opposed to the heaviness (I do not say, nor mean, 'unimportance') of doctrinal or propositional accuracy. It was also the commandment (two commandments, if we are to be mathematically strict) that Jesus singled out in response to a scribal question about the most important of the 613 commandments of the Law (Mark 12:29-31), namely love of God and love of neighbour.

Signs of hope

We should not, however, despair in the face of these obstacles. There are signs in our world of a renewed openness to other Christians, and not just on the part of the leaders of the churches. Very often this openness surfaces when Christians of different denominations find themselves working on a common project, and discover how close they are to each other. In my years of working in South Africa, just as apartheid was ending, I recall frequently being told how people who found themselves in prison because their Christianity had led them to oppose apartheid, discovered other such Christians, who sang the same hymns, acted in the same way, and regarded Jesus as Lord, and realised how close they were to each other. I can also recall a Catholic outstation, high in the Natal hills, where on those Sundays when the priest could not come to say mass, the people would join the services of the Methodists or Anglicans to praise God (and, incidentally, sing the same hymns). Many people in South Africa also recall the indispensable Christian input, led by the redoubtable Archbishop Tutu, to the Truth and Reconciliation Commission in that country, which did such great work. I also remember well how Dutch Reformed attitudes to Catholics

---

29. Homily 7, 8 on 1 John, Migne *Patrologia Latina* (PL) 43:23-32 [3].
30. 'Love – and then do what you desire' is one possible translation.

seemed to me to have altered from the suspicion I thought I detected among dominies when I first arrived to work in South Africa (though that suspicion may also, of course, have been because I was English). Twelve years later, there was tangible interest in what the Catholic tradition might have to offer to other Christians, notably in the area of sacramentality and spirituality. Since then, time spent teaching in Oxford and in Boston, Massachusetts, has continued to reveal something of the same: a renewed openness to religion, an impatience with Christian divisions, and, I noticed, an increasing number of people from other Christian traditions who have been looking for spiritual accompaniment, even from one who was not only Catholic but also Jesuit.

Another sign of hope has emerged in recent years from the Theology Faculty at Durham University in England, which gives to this new theological movement the helpful title of 'receptive ecumenism',[31] echoed in Walter Kasper's comment that, 'This receptivity to the present and the future is crucial today with respect to ecumenism.'[32] This is a line to pursue in the years ahead; and it does not oblige us to abandon our central perceptions, though it may compel us to reconsider exactly what we mean by them and how other Christians may understand our expression of them.

The need for Christians to work together

One of the things that we have to do, to which Pope Francis is constantly inviting us, is to keep our eyes on the state of the world, and where people are suffering, (what Francis calls the 'field hospital'[33]). You will be able to make your own list of issues, but at least in the following areas a united Christian voice would be more effective, simply in making the world a better place: human trafficking, religious persecution, the plight of refugees, and the abuse of our planet. There is also, of course, the problem of what you might call 'the death of God', the new atheism, the abandonment of moral standards (in the world of banking might be one example, but there are others), and the exodus from the churches in Europe and to some extent in North America; and, a problem coming from the opposite direction, the angry fundamentalism of some religious people.[34] Working together in the face of these problems will not only have a striking effect on our world, but will also reveal to us how much we have in common.

---

31. See the articles cited in the bibliography by Avis and Murray; and compare what Hurley says, apparently independently, on p.51 of *Christian Unity*, about 'reception' and 'receptivity'.
32. Quoted in Sachs, *Catholicism in a New Key*, p.175.
33. In the well-known interview with Antonio Spadaro, available at: http://www.lastampa.it/2013/09/19/vaticaninsider/eng/the-vatican/antonio-spadaro-interviews-francis-the-church-is-a-field-hospital-where-wounds-are-treated-ZrRM4dLcOYJ2bpR8x9gvWI/pagina.html (accessed 9 December 2016).
34. On issues of this sort, see James Carroll, *Christ Actually* (Viking, 2014).

Living in love

Finally (and I have to say that I advance this point with some hesitation, fearful of rolling eyes and the exclamation, 'Not that old business again!'), we have to live in love with each other. We are invited, that is to say, to show generous respect each to the other. We are invited to approach our fellow Christians with the attitude of 'what are your questions?' rather than the more peremptory 'these are my answers'. We have, too, to recognise that diversity is not the opposite of unity, and that what we are looking for is what Walter Kaspar calls 'reconciled diversity'. That is what Catholicism means, an umbrella that embraces all those for whom Jesus Christ is Lord.

Conclusion

And how are we to do this? Let me offer some generalisations, in the certainty that unless we operate in some such way as this we shall not succeed in our endeavour. We have to listen out for God's word; we have to keep our eyes on Jesus; we have to follow the leading of the Spirit. If we do that, we shall find three things happening to us: first, we shall, quite naturally, work together on local ecumenical projects, such as Christians are doing all over the world and all through history. Second, we shall, as a matter of course, find ourselves praying together. Thirdly, and this may be the tricky bit, it will seem entirely appropriate to engage together in theological investigation, to try to articulate where we agree and disagree. Then, without any surrender of insights that really matter, we may find that what divides us is indeed far less significant than those apparently daunting sources of division, and so we shall respond to Jesus' prayer to his Father in the Last Supper discourse, 'that they may be one as we are one' (John 17:22).

Do we have to give up what is precious to us? Not in the sense that we have to surrender hard-won doctrinal insights. But we may have to surrender our lovelessness, and recognise that love trumps doctrine.

CHAPTER 2

Paul and the Paulines on divisions

The overall argument of this chapter is quite simple: that for Paul unity is a value to be cherished, and that he gets irritated when people do not show a high esteem for it. Look, for example, at this text, from 1 Corinthians 11:16. Paul has just run through about five arguments in favour of his position that women should pray or prophesy with their heads covered, and, perhaps dimly aware that he may not be carrying the Corinthians with him, he concludes with the following acerbic comment:

> But if someone wants to pick a fight, we do not have any practice of this sort – and neither do the churches of God!

We have no way of telling what effect this argument had on his correspondents, but we need to be aware that Paul knew of the dangers of division, and that his Christians, especially his Corinthian Christians, needed to do something about it. We shall, however, leave those feuding Corinthians, and their Roman counterparts, until the next chapter. For the moment, we shall look at the remaining Pauline writings, in the order in which they appear in your Bibles.[35]

Galatians

Galatians is by some way the angriest of Paul's surviving letters; the reason he is so cross with the Christians in Galatia is that they have given in to the divisive tactics of conservative fundamentalists who are challenging Paul's radical views on the need for circumcision; we should notice that terrible remark at 5:12: 'I hope that those who are disturbing you may castrate themselves'. His solution is, as always, that they must keep their eyes on Christ. So, right at the beginning, he insists (1:7) on 'the gospel of Christ', which is at all costs not to be perverted; then at 1:11, 12 he reiterates the point, and underlines that it was Christ who gave Paul the gospel: 'the gospel that was gospelled by me is not of human origin. For I did not receive it from a human being, nor was I taught. No – it came from a revelation of Jesus Christ.' At the heart of the matter is the threat to the Galatians' freedom in Jesus Christ (2:4); Paul's concern is that they are not to be enslaved. It is possible, of course, that we shall find ourselves reflecting

---

35. It may be helpful to know that the order of the Pauline letters is dictated not by the order in which they were written, but by their length (Romans longest, Thessalonians shortest), and by putting letters to churches ahead of letters to individuals.

that Paul may not be doing a great deal for the cause of Christian unity by some of the language that he uses here ('because of some pseudo-Christians who had been smuggled in, who sneaked in to spy on our freedom which we have in Christ Jesus, in order to make slaves of us'); but clearly the issue is one that he regards as being of immense importance.

The answer to the problem of their divisions is, as it must always be, that the Galatians are to keep their eyes on Christ. Look at 2:16:

> Knowing that a person is not justified by performing the Law,
> but only by faith in Jesus Christ,[36]
> and we have come to faith in Jesus Christ,
> so that our justification is the result of faith in Christ,
> not about performing the Law.
> You see, no human being is justified by performing the Law.

The central point here is not what is sometimes called 'the doctrine of justification by faith'; it is rather that what counts is keeping Christ in the centre of our vision. All that matters is commitment to Jesus. This is emphasised by the explosive verse 3:1:

> You *foolish* Galatians![37]
> Before whose eyes Jesus Christ was publicly portrayed as crucified . . .

It is hard to know what we are to understand by this; generally, it is taken as a hint of how powerful was Paul's preaching. My sense of it, however, is that it may have been some kind of mystical experience that Paul shared with his Galatians, and which they and he could not deny. The central point, though, is clearly that they must continue to keep their eyes on Jesus. And if we get that right, then divisions are impossible. Consider the implications of 3:27, 28, where Paul is exploring with his Galatians the implications of baptism, in which for Paul, using a metaphor from the stage, we 'put on' Christ, when we are baptised 'into Christ'. And the upshot is that all the artificial categories that we use to 'label' people are utterly irrelevant:

> There is [in him] no such thing as
> Jew or Greek,
> No such thing as slave or free,
> No such thing as male and female.
> For you are all one in Christ Jesus.

---

36. or: 'the faith *of* Jesus Christ'.
37. An eminent colleague translates this as 'you crazy Celts'. (The late John Ashton, in a private communication).

Consider these three pairs; each of them states that there are two different kinds of human being: the first division is on the basis of racial and religious differences, the second rests on socio-political and economic factors, and the third on gender (when Paul speaks of male and female, by the way, he is deliberately referring back to the way God created humanity, according to Genesis 1:27). So where God creates a unity, human beings may not create divisions. For God is a unity, and our task is to keep our eyes on the 'dance' that is the richness of God, as Paul explains, a few verses later: 'because[38] you are [God's] children, God sent the Spirit of his Son into our hearts, crying out "Abba, Father"'. This utterance obviously quotes Jesus' prayer in Gethsemane (at least according to Mark 14:36) and stresses the undividedness of God, and underlines where our attention needs to be, if we are to radiate both the richness of God and God's undividedness.

Another metaphor that Paul uses in order to bring an end to the Galatians' divisions is that of the 'slave'. We have already said that Galatians is about freedom, as opposed to slavery, but this has an ingenious twist on it, in that the Galatians are to become slaves of each other (5:13):

> You were called into freedom, brothers and sisters;
> but [beware]: not freedom as giving sinfulness its opportunity.
> No – through love, you are to be slaves to each other.

Once we see our task in that light, then the idea of divisions is put firmly in its place. Otherwise the effect on the community can be utterly destructive: 'If you bite each other [*bite* each other? What *were* those Galatians doing?] and devour each other, watch out – you might be destroyed by each other' (5:15). We should do well to recite those words to ourselves today.

In the final chapter of the letter (6:1), Paul gives us an excellent rule for coping with divisions, which we should do well to observe in our own time and place:

> Brothers and sisters, if a person is caught in some transgression,
> you who are spiritual are to put that person right,
> but in a spirit of gentleness, keeping an eye on yourselves,
> in case you get tempted too.

And above all, we are not to prioritise our own interests, but those of the other (6:2-5):

> Carry one another's burdens; and that's how you're going to fill up the law of Christ.
> For if someone thinks they are something, when they are nothing,
> they are deceiving themselves.

---

38. or, just possibly, 'as a sign that'.

So let each one assess their own works,
And then their boasting will be with regard to themselves alone,
and not with regard to the other.

Paul offers two 'lists', what he calls the 'works of the flesh' (5:18-21) in contrast to the 'fruit of the Spirit' (5:22, 23). We shall do well to reflect on these two lists in our dealings with each other, and ask what is the tone of our relationships with other Christians.

Works of the flesh	Fruit of the Spirit
Fornication	Love
Impurity	Joy
Debauchery	Peace
Worshipping idols	Patience
Doing drugs	Kindness (note that the Greek word would sound like Christlikeness)
Animosities	Goodness
Strife	Faithfulness
Jealousy	Meekness
Rage	Self-control
Selfish ambition	
Dissension	
Factionalism	
Envy	
Drunkenness	
Carousing – and all that sort of thing	

Ephesians

Ephesians is a remarkable letter, and it is all about unity. The basic argument concerns what God has done in Christ, namely to overcome all that divides us. There is a problem about authorship, in that most scholars nowadays seem to agree that Paul did not write the letter; but if it was not Paul himself, then it was clearly someone who understood him well.

At the heart of the matter is a very high doctrine of the Church, the Church Universal rather than local, over which Christ is the head (1:22, 23); here the author is developing the idea of the Church as body of Christ that is already present in 1 Corinthians and Romans, as well as the letter to the Colossians, which in many ways runs close to Ephesians. The one body is composed of both Jews and Gentiles (a very deep division in that first-century world), whom Christ 'reconciled, both of them, in one body to God through the Cross, putting the hostility to death by means of [the Cross]' (2:16). So unity is an underlying theme in this letter, and (as always with Paul) he stresses the importance of love (see 3:17, 19).

There is one very important passage (4:1-7) in which Paul deals, rather ingeniously, with the question of unity, playing on the word 'one'. The translation that follows is an attempt to catch the flavour, including using bold and italics for the word *one*, though it makes for a certain clumsiness:

> So I am begging you, I who am a prisoner in the Lord,
> to behave in a manner that is worthy of the calling [in] which you were called
> with all humility and weakness, with patience,
> putting up with each other in love,
> being eager to preserve the *one*ness of the Spirit
> in the uniting power of peace.
> There is *one* body and *one* Spirit,
> just as you were called in *one* hope of your calling,
> *one* God and Father of all, who is over all and through all and in all,
> and to each *one* of us the grace was given
> in accordance with the measure of Christ's free gift.

Then he goes back to 1 Corinthians 12:12-31 and meditates on the significance of the idea of Christ's body for unity.

There is one other passage in Ephesians that it seems important to mention in this context, namely the so-called 'household code', which you will find at 5:21–6:9. When you read it, you may find yourself saying, possibly with just a hint of indignation, 'but if Paul is envisaging a society where the men are superior to the women and the parents are superior to the children, and absolutely everyone is superior to the slaves, what's the cash-value of all this talk about unity in the midst of divisions?'

Let us read the text together.

> [Be] *subordinated to each other, in reverence for Christ,*
> the women to their own husbands as to the Lord,
> because the man is the head of the woman,
> just as Christ is the head of the Church
> (he is Saviour of the body),
> so just as the Church is subordinated to Christ,
> so the women to their husbands in every respect.

Husbands – love your wives,
just as Christ loved the Church, and handed himself over for her sake,
in order to make her holy, purifying her with the washing of water by a word,
in order that he might offer himself the Church, in splendour,
with not a single blemish or wrinkle, or anything of that sort,
that she might be holy and spotless.
This is how the men ought to love their own women,
just like their own bodies.
If a man loves his wife, he is loving himself.
You see, no one hates their own flesh: no – they nourish and cherish it,
just as Christ does with the Church;
because we are limbs of his body –
that is why a man will abandon his father and mother
and stick to his wife – and the two become a single flesh.
This is a great mystery; and I am speaking of Christ and of the Church.
But each of you males is to love your own wife as yourself,
and the woman should revere the man.

Now as for children: you are to obey your parents in the Lord. For that is right.
'Honour your father and mother', which is the first commandment in the promise,
'that it may be well with you, and you may have a long life in the land'.

Now as for you parents: you are not to provoke your children:
instead you are to bring them up with the Lord's discipline and admonition.

Now as for you who are slaves: you are to obey your 'lords-according-to-the-flesh',
with fear and trembling and with generosity of heart,
as though you were obeying Christ,
not serving-to-catch-the-eye, or to-please-human-beings,
no: as Christ's slaves, doing the will of God from your heart,
slaving with generosity, as though for the Lord, not human beings.
Be aware that if anyone does a good deed, they will get a reward from the Lord,
whether they are slave or free.

Now as for you 'slave-lords': you are to do the same for them,
and give up threatening behaviour.
You must be aware that the Lord, your Lord as well as the Lord of your slaves,
is in heaven. And there is no snobbery about him.

What can we say about all this? The first thing to notice is the first line, 'be subordinated to each other'. That is what dictates the teaching that is contained in the rest of the quoted text, that the inter-relationship of Christians should rest on the assumption that we are all there to serve one another.

Secondly, we notice that, on the face of things, Paul (or whoever wrote this) is buying into the patriarchal culture of the Graeco-Roman world in which it is written. Wives are to obey their husbands, children their parents, and slaves their owners; and these days a good many people find themselves getting very hot under the collar at the author of this text for approving a pyramidal society. They should read more carefully, however, because, as we shall see, the way our author constructs the passage is very subversive of these relations of dominance and subjugation.

Thirdly, it is far less about human relationships than about the overall context, which continues Ephesians' treatment of the mystery of what God has done in Christ; and we are evidently intended to read this particular text in the light of what the author says about the relationship between Christ and the Church.

Fourthly (again if you read attentively), the author carefully subverts each of these pairings. It is perfectly true that wives are told to obey their husbands; but it is essential not to overlook the other side of that equation, that husbands are to love their wives, and that is explained in terms of giving their lives for them, just as Christ did for the Church. It is also true that children are ordered to obey their parents, but in virtually the same breath, parents are told not to 'provoke' their children, but to 'bring them up' (the Greek word can mean 'feed' them). And likewise, slaves are told to 'obey' their slave-masters; but look carefully at the passage, and admire the skill with which the author plays with the idea of 'lords' for slave-masters, and relativises it and subordinates the apparent priority of bosses over slaves by insisting that both sides have one Lord, namely God in heaven. Now it may be that things had been going wrong in Christian communities, and they needed an admonishing word; but anyone who thinks that Paul simply endorses the superiority of men over women, adults over children, or indeed the existence of the slave trade, has simply not been paying attention.

Philippians

The church in Philippi, up there in Macedonia at the top end of Greece (see map on page 30) has a fair claim to be Paul's favourite group of Christians. They had been very generous to him when he was in need during his work in Thessalonica (4:15, 16); and (even though he is in prison) this letter is by some way Paul's most joyful composition. We are looking for evidence of divisions, however, and it is certainly to be met with here.

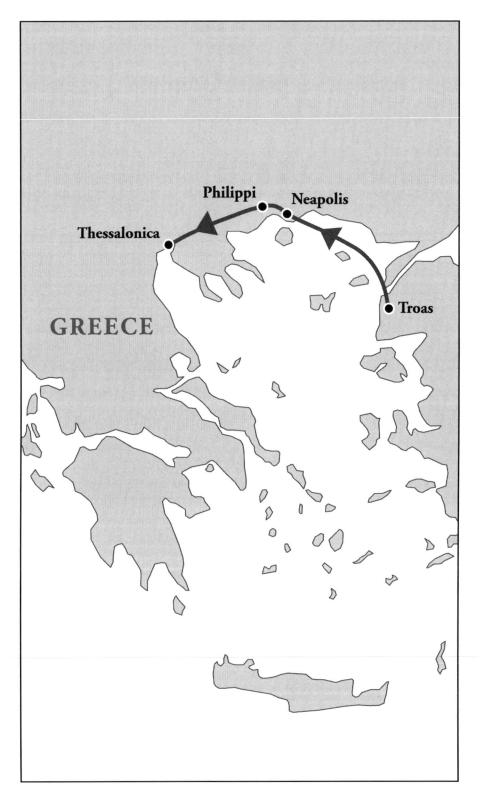

We start with what is on any reckoning very odd behaviour (1:13-18):

> My imprisonment has become well known in Christ,
> in the entire Praetorium and with everyone else.
> Most of the brothers and sisters in the Lord have taken confidence
> from my imprisonment to dare even more abundantly to speak the word.
> But some people preach through spite and discord,
> While some preach Christ out of goodwill.
> Some [do it] out of love, knowing that I am situated here
> for the defence of the gospel,
> others preach Christ out of self-seeking, not from motives of purity.
> They think that they are causing trouble for me in my imprisonment.
> So what? The only thing that matters is that in every way,
> whether out of pretence or out of sincerity, Christ is preached . . .

This is very strange indeed, and we do not really know what is going on, with some people preaching Christ in order to upset Paul in his imprisonment; but for our purposes, what is interesting is that there is clearly division within the Christian Church, and Paul, as always, copes by keeping his eyes on Christ. We do not know who these people were, who were preaching 'through spite and discord', but it is interesting evidence, in such a letter as this, of divisions in the early Church.

There are a few more straws in the wind. Everyone knows the great 'hymn to Christ' in chapter 2 (verse 5), where Paul exhorts the Philippians to 'Have the same mind-set which was in Christ Jesus, who being in the form of God . . .'; but it is worth looking at how he introduces the topic. He wants there to be:

> Consolation in Christ, the comfort of love, solidarity of the Spirit, compassion and mercy' and he asks them to 'fill out my joy by having the same mindset, the same love, of one mind, of the same mindset, doing nothing out of self-seeking [here, significantly, he repeats the word he had used back in chapter 1] or vainglory, but in humility thinking that others are their superiors. Not each one looking out for their own interests but each one for the others.
> *Philippians 2:1-4*

Presumably that is what they had not been doing in Philippi; and indeed we can go a little deeper into the matter, for in chapter 4 he repeats the phrase about 'having the same mindset in the Lord'. Here (4:2) he is talking about two ladies, Evodia and Syntyche, whom he greatly admires and who have 'fought at my side in the gospel', who are in some disagreement. We do not know what the disagreement was about, but clearly it was serious enough for it to have reached Paul's prison. (And it is just possible that the 'noble yoke-fellow' who is addressed in that verse, and asked to assist them, may have been Mrs Paul, which would be an interesting sidelight on the question of Christian unity.)

We should also notice, of course, that Paul himself can be divisive. We have already noted his dreadful remark to the Galatians linking circumcision and castration (Galatians 5:12); now listen to this: 'look out for the dogs, look out for the evil-doers, look out for the circumcision', for another remark that many of his readers will have found offensive (Philippians 3:2).

It is a lovely letter, this to the Philippians; but it brings with it evidence of the divisions in the early Church, and the ways that they developed to cope.

Colossians

Our next letter also carries evidence of division. When the author (who may or may not have been Paul) tells his audience that he hopes that 'no one should delude you with plausible arguments' (2:4), we do not know who he has in mind; but he does, and presumably his audience is well aware of what he is talking about. They will know what he means when he expresses the hope that they would be 'rooted in and built upon him, and made secure in faith as you have been taught' (2:7); but clearly it refers to possible division. This is even clearer in what follows: 'Watch out that no one kidnaps you through philosophy and empty deceit, in accordance with the tradition of human beings, in accordance with the elements of the world, and not in accordance with Christ' (2:8). Do you see, once more, how the answer to their divisions is for them to keep their eyes on Christ? As in Philippians, interestingly enough, so here the next move is into a great hymn about Christ: 'In him dwells the whole fullness of the Godhead, in bodily form . . .' (2:9-15).

So what the Colossians have to do is to work out what really matters. He gives an example of this at 2:16-19:

> So don't let anyone condemn you on matters of food or drink
> or in respect of a festival or new moon or Sabbath.

If we are honest, we cannot be certain what the dispute here is about, but clearly there was one, and so this is yet another example of divisions in the early Church, possibly a dispute with some group of Jewish Christians. For our purposes it is enough to note that there are divisions and that the answer is to keep eyes on Christ, who is 'the head' (2:10), and to whom belongs the 'body' [or, possibly, the 'reality'] (2:19), and with whom Christians may be said to have 'died to the elements of the world' (2:20).

There is further evidence of division in the stress laid on the importance of mutual forgiveness (3:12, 13):

So put on, as chosen ones of God, holy and beloved,
bowels of mercy,
kindliness,
humble attitudes,
meekness,
patience,
putting up with one another, and forgiving one another
when anyone has a grievance,
just as the Lord forgave you, that is what you are to do.

Once again, we see the insistence on putting an end to divisions and keeping the eyes on what the Lord has done.

Then there are those household codes (3:18-4:1). We have already looked at the equivalent passage in Ephesians, and it is not necessary to repeat what we said there. For us, the bottom line is 3:16, 17, which gives the priority to Christ, and then introduces the codes:

Let the word of Christ live abundantly in you.
You should teach and admonish each other with all wisdom,
with psalms and hymns and spiritual songs,
singing with gratitude in your hearts to God.
So everything that you do, whether it is speech or action,
let everything happen in the name of the Lord Jesus,
in gratitude to God the Father through him.

That is the tone in which our author then enters upon the household codes and the commands about how husbands and wives, children and parents, slaves and their masters, are to behave towards one another. Once again, the way to cope with potential divisions here is for the Colossians (and us) to keep their (and our) eyes upon Jesus and upon God.

1 Thessalonians

The next text in your Bibles is almost certainly the first New Testament document to be written, what we call the first letter to the church in Thessalonica up there in Macedonia, along the road from Philippi (have a look at the map on page 30). And even here (2:4-8) we can see hints of divisions (though it must be said that this is for the most part a very loving letter):

> ... as we were approved by God to be entrusted with the gospel,
> that is how we speak, not trying to curry favour with human beings,
> but trying to please God who approves our hearts.
> For we never turned up with a flattering speech, as you are well aware,
> nor trying to cover up greed (God is my witness).
> Nor were we looking for human glory, whether from you or from anyone else,
> throwing our weight around as apostles of Christ.
> No – we were like infants among you,
> just like a nurse nourishes her own children.
> That is how we loved you, and were happy to share with you,
> not only the gospel of God, but even our own lives
> – because you had become beloved by us.

Paul is inclined to be defensive in the face of criticism, and we may detect here a hint of possible accusations laid against him in Thessalonica, which might be evidence for certain divisions.

In the next chapter we hear the same tone once more (3:10-13):

> Night and day we begged to see your face,
> and to make up what was lacking in your faith.
> May our God and Father direct our journey to you.
> May the Lord make you abound and overflow in love for each other and for all
> (just as we love you),
> so as to strengthen your hearts and make them blameless in holiness
> before our God and Father in the presence of our Lord Jesus
> with all his saints.
> Amen.

Is it overdoing it here to detect Paul defending himself against certain allegations, which are hinted at in these lines? There may be further evidence here for divisions in the Church in the very first document to be written in the New Testament, as in the exhortation almost at the end of the letter (5:13-15): 'live at peace with one another. We beg you, brothers and sisters, admonish those who are disorderly, comfort those who are fainthearted, be concerned for the sick and be patient with everybody.' Here too, in the exhortation to look after even the least promising, there may be a hint of certain divisions that Paul had heard about, or at least thought possible, in the church at Thessalonica. The point is, you see, that Paul is reacting to actual situations that arose in the early Church, so we can feel in what he writes some traces of disputes among them.

2 Thessalonians

One of the problems about 2 Thessalonians is that many scholars feel that it could not have been written by Paul, mainly because it is hard to find a convincing historical setting for it. For our purposes it is sufficient to observe that the author is dealing with the problem that some people, thinking that Jesus might be returning any day now, were doing no work at all, and for them the rule had to be introduced: no work, no food (3:10)!

There are other indications of division. At 1:8 there is a reference to 'those who do not obey the gospel of our Lord Jesus'. At 2:2 the author gives a warning 'not to be shaken' by a message of any sort (spirit, word, letter apparently coming from us) to the effect that 'the day of the Lord has come'. So there are divisions there, and there is even (3:14) a mention of the possibility of excommunication: 'if a person does not obey our word through this letter, identify this one, as someone not to have dealings with'. But we should notice the reason: 'that he may be put to shame – and don't think of the person as an enemy, but admonish them as a fellow Christian'. Excommunication is enormously tempting, and we have all had fantasies of reaching for a papal bull to get rid of someone in the church whom we cannot stand; but we should be very careful indeed before taking such a final option.

The Pastoral Letters

What we call the 'Pastoral Letters' are those which come almost last in the Pauline collection, two to Timothy and one to Titus. They are called 'pastoral' presumably because they are addressed to two church leaders ('pastor' is simply the Latin word for shepherd). Incidentally, you will often find the claim made that the letters were first so named by eighteenth-century scholars; but in fact it was St Thomas Aquinas.[39] Most scholars nowadays are of the view that they were not written by Paul, but by a later follower.[40]

For our purposes, what is of interest is that they show a developing institutionalisation. Now this is almost always a 'boo' word in church circles, but developing as an institution is something that must come, sooner or later, even to the most charismatic churches, if they are to survive. So there are instructions

---

39. He describes 1 Timothy as 'a rule, so to say, for pastors' (Comm. Super I Epist. ad Tim. lectio ii in 1:3). I am indebted to Professor Pheme Perkins for this observation, in a private communication.
40. It is a curious fact that a good many phrases from these pastoral letters have found their way into Christian hymnody. You might like to make a list of familiar ideas as you read.

about the right sort of people to appoint as 'episkopos' (a word that originally means something like 'overseer', but eventually turns into our word 'bishop') at 3:1-7;[41] then there are those who can be safely appointed as 'deacon' (which really means 'servant'), whose ideal qualities are listed at 3:8-12; and 'widows' (a term that at present has no institutional equivalent in the Church) – you will find the kind of virtues to be expected of them at 5:3-16. Likewise there are elders ('presbyters', the word that eventually turns into our 'priests'), about whom some general remarks are made at 5:17-24.

And there are clear signs of divisions. At 1 Timothy 1:4-7 we read of 'stories and endless genealogies', and some people who have 'missed the mark and turned away to useless talk'. Then we hear (1:19, 20) of Hymenaeus and Alexander, whom the author has 'handed over to Satan that they may be educated not to blaspheme'. We have no idea who these two were, or what their punishment might have been. Our task here is to notice the evidence for divisions in that community, but also to notice that the sanction invoked implies that they will come back to their right minds.

At 6:1, 2 there is an exhortation to mutual respect in the Church (in this case between slaves and their masters), which presumably means that there was a problem in that area. The verses immediately following (6:3-5) help us to understand what might have been going wrong: 'teaching different things, not approaching the health-giving words of our Lord Jesus Christ . . . envy, strife, blasphemy, wicked conjectures, the quarrelling of mentally corrupted people, who are deprived of the truth, and think that you can make money out of self-sufficient piety'. It does not at all matter that we cannot confidently pin down what the trouble was. The person(s) to whom this letter was addressed will presumably have understood. The point as far as we are concerned is that there was trouble of a significant sort in the Church, and that it had to be dealt with.

The same is true of 2 Timothy. So at 1:15 we read again that there has been trouble: 'Phygelos and Hermogenes have abandoned me'. At 2:14 there is mention of the dangers of 'useless fighting with words', though the precise meaning remains rather obscure; at 2:17 more names are named: Hymenaeus and Philetos, of whom it is said that their message is 'like gangrene'. It seems that they have been preaching that 'the resurrection has already happened'. Names are named again at 4:10, 14, where it is Demas, Crescens, Titus, and Alexander who have abandoned the author.

Likewise in Titus, the third 'pastoral letter', there is trouble afoot, for at 1:10, 11 we learn that 'there are many who are rebellious, talking empty nothings and deceiving people's minds . . . They have to be silenced; they teach entire

---

41. Compare Titus 1:7-9.

households, for the sake of immoral profit.' And, finally, at 3:9 we read of 'foolish debates and genealogies and quarrels about the Law'. It is impossible at this stage to reconstruct them; this sort of thing could be said at any stage in the Church's history. There is nothing new about our divisions.

Philemon

Now we come to the last of the Pauline letters. Unlike some of the others we have looked at, this was certainly written by Paul. It is a charming little postcard of a letter, and when I teach a course on Paul, I very often start with it. The letter has a very strong sense of the solidarity that should exist among Christians. Paul is asking a big favour of Philemon, on behalf of Onesimus, who is probably a runaway slave – namely, that Philemon should accept him as a brother in Christ, not as a miscreant to be punished. The underlying point, possibly edged out by the social, political and economic relationship between Onesimus and his owner, is that 'we are all Christians together', a point that underlines Paul's argument in verse 20.

Conclusion

In this chapter, we have been eavesdropping on some of the difficulties of the Church of the first century. There is nothing new about our divisions; dissension is not an invention of later centuries, but has always been there in the Church, and the obligation is upon us to do something about it.

CHAPTER 3

Divisions in Paul's Corinthian and Roman correspondence

The Corinthian correspondence

The underlying problem in 1 Corinthians is that the Christians in Corinth are divided, and Paul does not like it at all. So this is a very good place for us to look at the questions of divisions in the early Church; in this chapter, therefore, we shall look principally at 1 Corinthians, and then more briefly at 2 Corinthians and Romans.

Eyes on Jesus

In the first of these important letters, the theme of divisions starts very early indeed. If the Corinthians were listening carefully when the document was being read out to them, they would have noticed two things at once: first, that the name of Jesus, or Christ, or any combination of these, is used is no fewer than ten times in the first ten verses. Here, once again, we see the solution to divisions in the Church (though the lesson is not precisely stated): keep your eyes on Jesus (and also on God, of course, who is mentioned five times).

The use of the passive voice

Secondly, if you will forgive a tedious grammatical observation, they may have noticed the number of passives used in these verses (which I have printed in *italics*, with the subtle implication (not explicitly made at this point) that all the qualities that the Corinthians have are gifts that *have been given* them, not something on which they can pride themselves. Paul starts this idea in verse 1, referring, diplomatically enough, to himself: '*called as an apostle* of Christ Jesus through the will of God'. Then he applies it to the Corinthian Christians, who '*have been made holy*', and '*called to be saints*' (v.2). Then he reminds them that it is 'God's free *gift*'[42] (the word is often translated as 'grace') 'which *was given* to you in Christ Jesus' (v.4); and the pattern continues in verse 5: 'you *have been made rich* in every respect in him in all rhetoric and all knowledge' (here he lists two qualities on which the Corinthians prided themselves; and they

---

42. This is of course an implicit passive.

were slightly contemptuous of Paul that he lacked them). He goes on in the same vein: 'the witness of Christ *has been made strong* in you, so that you lack in no free *gift* as you await the revelation of our Lord Jesus Christ' (vv.6, 7) and emphasises that 'he will strengthen you to the end, *irreproachable* [in the Greek, this is another unmistakably passive form] to the end' (v.8), before he concludes the introduction: 'God is faithful, through whom you *have been called* into the solidarity of his son Jesus Christ our Lord'. If those Corinthians were really paying attention, they may have asked themselves why he was emphasising not how wonderful they are, but how much God in Christ had done for them. That, by the way, is even today a good way of coping with all our divisions.

The cult of personality

After that unusually subtle approach (Paul is normally a bit more direct), he gets more explicitly down to business, asking them to sort out their divisions: 'I am begging you, brothers and sisters, through the name of our Lord Jesus Christ, that you all say the same, and that there be not divisions,[43] and that you be repaired in the same mind and in the same disposition. For it has been revealed to me by Chloe's people[44] that there are quarrels among you.' Then Paul lets them know what precisely he means – there has been a cult of personalities: 'each of you says, "I am for Paul", or "I am for Apollos", or "I am for Kephas"'.[45] Then Paul counters this with his own grim little joke: 'Well – I am for Christ.' This insistence on 'eyes on Jesus' is presumably meant to bring all divisions to an end (although you might want to argue that, if that is indeed the case, he could sign off the letter here).

Paul's strategy is to stop them playing the cult of personality, and to get them thinking about Jesus instead: 'Is Christ divided? Was it Paul who was crucified on your behalf? Were you baptised in the name of Paul?' (v.13). Unfortunately, he now slightly spoils the effect by revealing some confusion. He wants to argue, presumably to avoid them starting a 'Paul' faction, that he 'did not baptise any of you' (v.14). Then it looks as though someone reminds him that in fact he had baptised 'Crispus and Gaius', and then he drives on with his argument 'so that no one should say that you were baptised in my name'. But then he had apparently to be reminded of some other people whom he had baptised: 'and

---

43. The Greek word for this is *schismata*, which is what 'scissors' do; it is an interesting fact that 50 per cent of the New Testament uses of this word are to be found in 1 Corinthians; although you may feel a bit disappointed that there are only six of them – the other three are in John's Gospel.
44. Alas, we have no idea who Chloe was, though it is a fair enough guess that she may have been a Christian shipping magnate whose 'people' plied their vessels between Corinth and Ephesus, where the letter is being dictated. If you listen very carefully, you can hear some of those Corinthians snarling, 'We're going to get that Chloe.'
45. The Aramaic version of the Greek name 'Peter', or 'Rock'.

I also baptised the house of Stephanas – but otherwise I don't think I baptised anyone else', and this slightly weakens the rhetorical effect.

Nothing daunted, however, Paul presses on with the argument, and with some determination tries to put in their place the personalities around whom Corinthian divisions might have been crystallising (and you might like to reflect on the equivalent today in church situations that you know, of personalities around whom divisions can arise). He concludes with a strong statement of what really matters, reminding them of his miserable arrival in Corinth (2:1-3):

> When I came to you, brothers and sisters, I came not with any excess of eloquence or cleverness, when I proclaimed to you God's mystery. You see, I had decided to know nothing among you except Jesus Christ – and him crucified! And I had arrived in weakness and fear and in much trembling.[46]

First and probably foremost there is the character of Apollos, and it may be that this was the trickiest problem of all. We know from Acts 18:24-8 that Apollos was an Alexandrian Jew, and an 'eloquent man ... strong in Scripture, instructed in the way of the Lord, and very enthusiastic in the Spirit', who was 'teaching and speaking accurately about Jesus; but he only knew John's baptism'. Then (v.26) Paul's friends Priscilla and Aquila came across him 'speaking confidently in the synagogue', and gave him some remedial theology lessons. Apollos later went across to Corinth, and it is a sensible guess that his Alexandrian eloquence[47] was compared very favourably with Paul's drier approach. So Paul above all wants to sort out the relationship between the two of them, and to insist that what matters is Christ (3:5):

> What is Apollos?
> What is Paul?
> They are *servants*, through whom you came to faith ...

Then he explores two metaphors for their function in the Church. The first is the metaphor of gardening (3:6-9):

> I planted, Apollos irrigated – but it was God who gave the growth.
> So neither the planter matters, nor the irrigator,
> but [only] God who gives the growth.
> The planter and the irrigator are on the same level,
> and each one will get their own reward for their own labour.
> For we are God's co-workers.

---

46. See Acts 17:32–18:1 for his less than triumphant departure from Athens to Corinth, which might account for the trembling. And Corinth was not the sort of city where he might expect to be successful.
47. The Alexandrians were known for their colourful exegesis of the scriptures.

Then he brings in both metaphors together (3:9):

> You are God's field, God's building.

This enables him to explore the second metaphor, that of a building project (3:10-15):

> By the grace of God that was given me,
> like an experienced architect I put down the foundation,[48]
> and someone else built on top of that,
> and everyone must look to see how they build on top.
> You see, no one can put down any other foundation than the one that is there,
> which is Jesus Christ.[49]
> Whatever someone builds on top of the foundation:
> gold, silver, precious stones, wood, grass or stubble,
> each one's work will become evident,
> for The Day will show it,
> because it is revealed by fire:
> and the fire will test it.
> If someone's work remains, what they have built on top,
> that person will get a reward.
> But if that person's work is destroyed by fire,
> the person will pay for it, though he himself will be saved,
> but as it were through fire.

The alert reader will notice that Paul does not hold out much hope for the survival of Apollos' work, as Paul resumes the argument (3:21-3, after a good deal of contrasting the 'wise' and the 'foolish'):

> So no one is to boast of human beings,
> for everything is yours,
> whether Paul or Apollos or Kephas,
> or the universe or life or death, or things present or things to come –
> all is yours;
> and you are Christ's and Christ is God's.[50]

Then he reaches the desired conclusion: 'so let a person regard us as servants of Christ and stewards of the mystery of God – and what you want from stewards

---

48. The reader will notice that Paul gently reminds the Corinthians that he got there first: it was he who planted, and he who did the ground-plan. Apollos, whom they so admire, came late on the scene.
49. Eyes, once again, on Jesus, you see, not on particular personalities.
50. Eyes, once more, on Christ and on God.

is that a person be found faithful'. So there are no grounds for getting 'puffed up' (4:6, 18) or for boasting (4:7) about different figures in the Church.

Apollos appears once more in the letter, at 16:12. At this point, Paul is into his farewell greetings. As we shall shortly see, after telling the Corinthians of his travel plans (16:5-9), he makes a mention of Timothy, before reverting to the ticklish question of Apollos, about whom he says the following (16:12):

> As regards brother Apollos, I begged him many times to come to you
> with the brothers and sisters.
> And it was absolutely not the will that he should come at present;
> but he will come when he gets a moment.

We have already seen that there is a tension over Apollos, and possibly Paul is seen by the Corinthians as an opponent of this gifted Alexandrian Jew. So here he is making it quite clear that they are in contact, and that it is not Paul (as the Corinthians may have suspected) who is preventing Apollos from paying a visit. Whose 'will' is it? Perhaps Paul is saying that Apollos did not want to come just now; or perhaps they had jointly discerned that it was not God's will. We can at all events see the tension here.

Then there is Timothy. We meet him first at 4:17, where (as we have seen) Paul has been encouraging the Corinthians to understand the roles of Apollos and himself; he more or less concludes this section by saying (4:16), 'I beg you to become imitators of me', and then continues:

> Because of this, I sent Timothy to you;
> he is my beloved child, and faithful in the Lord.
> He will remind you of my ways in Christ Jesus,
> just as I teach everywhere, in every church.

So the sending of Timothy has to do with an appropriate response to Paul (and presumably Apollos also), which Paul describes as being 'imitators'; this is the implication of 'remind you of my ways'. There is perhaps a hint that the Corinthians may not treat him very well, in the reference to Timothy being 'beloved' and 'faithful'. For there follows an unmistakable rebuke (4:18-20):

> Thinking that I was not coming to you, some people got puffed up.
> But I am going to come to you soon, and then I shall know about not the
> rhetoric of the puffed up ones, but their cash-value.
> For God's kingdom is not a matter of rhetoric but of cash-value.

Then comes a threat of corporal punishment; so clearly Paul regards this as a very important question, how they are to deal with Apollos, with Timothy, and with Paul himself (4:21):

> What are you after? Do you want me to come to you with a stick?
> Or with love and a spirit of gentleness?

Then, as we have said, Timothy reappears at the end; and Paul is evidently suspicious of the treatment that the Corinthians might mete out to him as Paul's representative (16:10, 11):

> And if Timothy comes to you, watch out that his visit is unafraid.
> For he is doing God's work just as I am.
> I don't want anyone to treat him with disdain.
> Send him peacefully on his way – that he may come to me.
> For I am expecting him, with the brothers and sisters.

Paul is clearly a bit worried; they might make Timothy afraid, possibly by saying 'we want the organ-grinder, not the monkey', failing to recognise that Timothy is Paul's emissary (and once again we notice the suggestion that they must keep their eyes on God). There is a hint of something of the sort at 1 Timothy 4:12 ('don't let anyone despise your youthfulness'); but it is hard to know what status to give this verse. And there is a firm reminder that Timothy is going to visit Paul after he has been to Corinth, so Paul will get a full report. Once again, we have a hint of personality clashes in Corinth.

Later in the chapter, we meet other personalities, and a suggestion of tensions, in the reference to Stephanas, Fortunatus and Achaicus (16:15-18):

> I am begging you, brothers and sisters: you know the household of Stephanas, Fortunatus and Achaicus. They are the first fruits of Achaia; and they have put themselves at the disposition of the saints, to serve them. I want you to be subordinated to people like this and to all my collaborators and fellow-workers.

These names, two Greek, and one Latin, are the kind of names that might be given to slaves (Fortunatus means something like 'Blessed', and Achaicus may indicate a person originating from Southern Greece, whose capital was Corinth), so it may well be that they are 'freedmen', or former slaves, and that some people in Corinth have been indicating that they don't want people of such low social status running things in their church. We have already found a reference to Stephanas, at 1:16, where Paul apparently required reminding that he had baptised Stephanas' household; that may be an indication that Stephanas is in Corinth with him. For our purposes all we need to notice is that there is tension here. Divisions are not unknown in the early Church, and especially at Corinth.

Images for unity: the Temple, the body

This may be the reason why Paul offers two images for unity in 1 Corinthians – namely, the idea of the Temple of God (3:16, 17; 6:19), and that of the body (6:19; 12:1-31). It may be useful to look at these two ideas before trawling through the rest of this letter for other instances of disunity.

This is how Paul presents the idea of the Temple. After his account of the role and status of himself and Apollos, and their relative unimportance, provided only that they build correctly, he goes on (3:16, 17):

> Don't you realise that you people are the Temple of God,
> and that the Spirit of God lives among you?
> If someone destroys the Temple of God, God will destroy that person.
> For God's Temple is holy – and that is you people.

The point here is that the cult of personality is destroying the church in Corinth and, as far as Paul is concerned, God regards that kind of division very seriously indeed. The holiness of the Church should mean that there is no in-fighting; for divisions function as a counter-statement, that the Church is unholy. If you find yourself saying at this point, 'Well nothing much has changed, then', you must make that a reason for doing something about the disunity in the present age.

The idea resurfaces at 6:19, this time in conjunction with our other image, that of the 'body', which is of great importance in later Pauline theology, as we saw with regard to Ephesians and Colossians:

> Do you not realise that your [plural] body is the Temple of the Holy Spirit among you, which you have from God, and that you do not belong to yourselves? For you were bought at a price. So glorify God in your body.

The context here is that some Christians in Corinth seem to have been giving in to the contemporary secular culture and making use of prostitutes (6:13). And Paul drifts from the individual body, which is used in intercourse with prostitutes ('don't you realise that your bodies are Christ's limbs?'), to the body that is the Church. The 'Temple' and 'the body' are images for the reality of the Christian community that is threatened by our divisions.

Paul then returns to the idea of the body as a metaphor for unity in chapter 12. The issue here is how to deal with 'spiritual gifts', on which the Corinthians evidently prided themselves. The criterion Paul offers is the attitude to Jesus: if you call Jesus 'Lord', then you are led by the Holy Spirit; but there is a further point, that there are different kinds of spiritual gifts, and they all belong together under God, and are all for the up-building of the Church. Paul lists some of them: 'clever rhetoric, rhetoric of knowledge, gifts of healing, working of miracles/powers, prophecy, discernment of spirits, different kinds of languages, and interpretation of languages', and Paul concludes that 'all these are worked by one and the same Spirit' (12:8-11). This then leads into the image of the body of Christ, which allows Paul to conjure up the humorous picture of different parts of the body declaring independence (12:15-17):

> If the foot says, 'I'm not a hand – I don't belong to the body', does that mean that it does not belong to the body?
> And if the ear says, 'I'm not an eye – I don't belong to the body', does that mean that it does not belong to the body? If the entire body were an eye, how would it hear? And if it were all hearing, how would it smell?

The point is that in the body of Christ, we all belong together (12:21):

> The eye cannot say to the hand, 'I have no need of you'.
> Nor again can the head say to the feet, 'I have no need of you.'

Then the argument goes a step further, dealing with the portions of the body that 'seem a bit weaker', but are necessary (12:22). These turn out (v.23) to be what an old British comedy series used to call 'the naughty bits', though Paul says of them (12:23-6):

> the bits of the body that we regard as less honourable; to these we give greater honour; and our indecent bits have greater decency. But our more decent bits have no need. No – God put the body together, giving more abundant honour to the bits that lacked it, so as not to have division[51] in the body, but on the contrary, all the parts having concern for one another. And if one part is suffering, all the parts suffer along with it; if one part is glorified, all the parts rejoice together.

Then Paul applies this to the church in Corinth (12:28-30):

> God placed some people in the church: first, apostles,[52] second prophets, third teachers, then miracles, then gifts of healing, help-giving, managerial

---

51. Our word 'schisma' once more.
52. You may observe that Paul is an apostle, and this group is placed first!

skills, and different kinds of languages.[53] We can't all be apostles, can we? Or all prophets? Or all teachers? Do all do miracles? Do all have the gift of healing? Do all speak in tongues? Do all interpret?

The point here is the very catholic one, that all belong together, with our very different gifts. And, oddly enough, precisely the possession of dramatic or striking gifts is very often a source of division in the Church; whenever you find yourself saying, 'I am more spiritual than X', watch out, for you are on the way to causing division. The gift of revering other parts of our body is one that we need today. Not all of us in the Church are the same, nor do we all have the same gifts. Catholicism should be a matter of recognising, and rejoicing in, the giftedness of others (but it is not easy).

Incest in church!

With all that in mind, we can look through the rest of this important letter, and see what we can find by way of evidence of division, and what remedies Paul offers. Once he has dealt with the cult of different personalities, he turns to sex; now sex is a wonderful gift from God, which in both the Corinth of his day and the world in which we live can be used to create division. The most obvious problem is that one of the members of the church in Corinth is living with 'his father's woman' (5:1). This is incest, and something that Paul regards as unsustainable in a Christian community, so the man has to be expelled (5:2). Although Paul, like Jesus his beloved master, preaches a gospel of freedom, that is not understood to mean that 'anything goes'. But it is important not to take this idea to extremes. We learn at 5:9 that in a previous letter Paul had told them not to have anything to do with those who are sexually immoral. Now in a city like Corinth, and, for all I know, in the city where you who are reading these words live, taking that literally might mean that you have no one to talk to at all ('you would have to go out of the world!', 5:10). But there is a serious point here and it is that, for Paul, you cannot share community with fellow Christians who do any of these things: 'the sexually immoral, the materially greedy, those who worship non-gods, slanderers, drunks, robbers – you are not even to eat with people like this'. Sometimes you feel that Paul gets a bit carried away with his lists of people, but the point is clear – that the Church needs to keep an eye on what company it keeps. Otherwise there will be divisions.

---

53. You will certainly observe that this gift, on which the Corinthians so prided themselves, is relegated to last place.

Litigation between Christians

And divisions there were aplenty in Corinth. The next source of division is that (to Paul's angry astonishment) some of them were taking each other to law. The arguments he uses against such an attitude are perhaps not as strong as he might wish, and certainly Christians down the centuries have not notably eschewed litigation with one another; but for our purposes, what is interesting is Paul's horror at their behaving in this way (6:1-8):

> One of you has the nerve, when he has an issue with someone else, to go to law, to the [courts of the] unjust and not the saints! Or are you not aware that it is the saints who are going to judge the world? . . . Christian goes to law with fellow Christian, and in the [courts of] unbelievers at that! It is already a defeat for you that you have lawsuits against each other. Would it not be better for you to suffer injustice? Would it not be better for you to let yourself be robbed? Instead, you people act unjustly and rob each other, Christians taking from other Christians!

It is worth sitting with this passage and recognising, possibly to our astonishment, that divisions in the Church are not, after all, a modern phenomenon.

What about sex?

Now I suggest that you turn to 7:1, that you take on board the fact that we are nearly halfway through this letter, and observe that it is only at this point that Paul condescends to answer the questions that they have posed to him in their (possibly rather complacent) letter. This may be Paul's way of reproving them for the serious things that they have got wrong rather than the somewhat trivial things that they are so pleased with having got right.

The issue here, once more (but this is Corinth), is, as it always must be, sex. The question has arisen, and it looks as though Paul is quoting back at an ascetically minded group in the city a slogan that they have produced, that 'it is good for a man not to touch a woman'. If that is the case, the question goes, can they even get married? The answer that Paul gives is that sex is indeed permissible, and that what matters is the context: they may abstain from sex, but only by common agreement, and only for a time, and then come back together again.

Then there is the question (7:8): 'what about the unmarried, and those who have not yet married?' To get the full flavour of it, we need to know the context, as the Corinthians certainly knew it, otherwise we may be giving Paul's answers to the wrong question. Then there are questions about what to do if your spouse is not a Christian, which Paul answers with some deftness, not insisting that they divorce, but allowing divorce or separation if the non-Christian partner wishes it. In the same chapter he deals with related questions about whether to change status: if they are circumcised, or uncircumcised, if they are slaves and have the chance to buy their freedom, basically Paul counsels such people to stay as they are. And if you find yourself getting indignant over this, then reflect on the situation; for Paul was of the view that the end might come soon ('the time is near the end', 7:29), and this means that there are more urgent questions afoot.[54] We cannot legislate for our own situation on the basis of what Paul says here; but we do need to notice, once more, that in Paul's day as in ours, there is division among Christians in good standing over matters of sex. In both our day and Paul's, the answer is, as it always must be, that we keep our eyes on the Lord (7:32-5):

> I want you to be trouble-free. For the unmarried person is troubled over the things of the Lord, how they are to please the Lord, while the person who has married is troubled about the things of the world, how they are to please their wife, and is divided. Likewise the unmarried woman and the virgin is troubled about the things of the Lord, to be holy in body and soul. Whereas the married woman is troubled about the things of the world, how to please her husband. Now I am telling you this for your advantage, not to put a noose on you, but in order [for things to be] orderly and devout, with no distractions.

The point here is not to legislate for our very different situation; rather we need to recognise that questions of sexual morality are potentially divisive, and that our way to solve them is not to shout each other down, so much as to keep our eyes on pleasing the Lord.

What about food offered to idols?

The next issue to surface is obviously an important one, since Paul's treatment of it covers no less than three chapters, 8 to 10. It is the question of the admissibility of eating food that has been offered to idols. At this point you may scratch your head and say that we don't have much of a problem with this in Aberdeen or Zululand; but just hold on. For anything that you put at the centre of your life, if it is not the real God, is going to let you down and leave you disillusioned. So idolatry needs to be taken seriously. In that world, there was a question of worshipping the wrong 'gods', Jupiter or Baal or Minerva, or whoever; in our world the gods are rather different (pleasure or prestige or money or power, roughly), but the topic remains potentially divisive.

---

54. There is no time for 'rearranging the deckchairs on the Titanic', as the cliché goes.

As he attempts to solve the problem, Paul reminds his hearers of the centrality of love. The Corinthians are claiming to have knowledge, to which Paul responds (8:1) that 'knowledge puffs up but love builds up'. That would not be a bad slogan for the whole of this letter. The problem of eating food offered to idols comes up in two ways. The first comes from a common practice in the ancient world – that when an animal is sacrificed to a god in a temple, the priests can sell off what remains of the carcass, which can then turn up in the market (see 10:25), and would represent a cheap way of getting protein. If this were the difficulty, then the problem would come from over-anxious religious people fearful that eating such food might count as worshipping false gods. The other way in which the question might arise is if a worshipper in the temple invites a Christian to join him for a meal in the temple dining-room, and a fellow Christian out for a walk looks inside and sees the Christian at supper, and leaps to the conclusion that he has abandoned the true religion.

Paul deals with this potentially divisive issue with admirable common sense. This is the heart of his teaching (8:4-6):

> With regard to eating food that has been offered to idols, we know that there is no idol in the world, and that there is no 'god' other than the One. For even if there are so-called 'gods', whether in heaven or on earth, just as there are many 'gods' and many 'lords', nevertheless,
> we have *one* God – the Father.
> From whom everything came to be, and we are for him,
> and *one* Lord – Jesus Christ.
> Through him everything came to be, and we are through him.

What Paul has done here is to take the great prayer of the Shema, recited twice a day by pious Jews, which speaks of 'the Lord your God', and divided it up, so that it speaks of 'God' and the 'Lord', to capture the richness of the Christian experience of God. Once you have seen that, then the relatively trivial question of eating the food is seen to be irrelevant. Nevertheless, there are others to think of (8:10-12):

> If someone sees you, who have knowledge, dining in an idol-house, might it not be the case that because he is weak, his conscience gets 'emboldened' to eat food that has been offered to idols? You see, your 'knowledge' destroys the one who is weak, your fellow Christian for whom Christ died. So when you sin against fellow Christians and batter their conscience, it is Christ you are sinning against.

Paul is repeating here the implications of his teaching about the 'body of Christ', which means that when you do damage to fellow Christians it is Christ whom you are damaging. (And the reader may recall Luke's version of the story of Paul's encounter with Jesus: 'Saul, Saul, why are you persecuting me?').

Then Paul comes to a conclusion about future policy (8:13):

Therefore, if food upsets my fellow Christian, I am not going to eat meat, ever, in order not to upset my fellow Christian.

Once again, the answer to the problem of division is: keep your eyes on Christ.

Paul's refusal to accept money

The next divisive issue is an unusual one, at least in our day, for Paul has been criticised because he refuses to accept money! The criticism of Christian leaders is normally on quite opposite grounds, that we are far too interested in getting our grubby paws on the people's hard-earned wealth; but, as Jewish rabbis and Congregationalist Christian ministers have shared with me, there is of course a certain freedom in not being paid by them.

This is how Paul puts it (9:4-6):

Do we not have freedom as regards food and drink?
Do we not have authority to take a Christian wife around with us, like the other apostles and the Lord's brothers, and Kephas?
Or is it just Barnabas and I who do not have authority not to work?

The point here is that apostles are entitled to make a living out of the gospel, 'But I did not use any of these [arguments]' (9:15). And the reason Paul did not make use of his freedom is that he has a 'need' to preach the gospel: 'woe to me if I do not preach the gospel' (9:16). And he continues, 'So what is my reward? It is that by preaching the gospel I make the gospel message free of charge, so as not to make use of the authority that is mine in the gospel' (9:18). So the answer to the divisions in Corinth about Paul's failure to accept their money (if this is the correct way of understanding this rather difficult passage) is the overriding importance of the gospel. And, incidentally, this is part of the answer to the whole question of eating food offered to idols: the overriding claim is that of the gospel of Christ; and that is the answer to all their, and our, divisions. Or, as Paul concludes at the end of his (not always absolutely easy) discussion of the problem, 'So – whether you are eating or drinking, or doing anything at all, do everything for the glory of God' (10:31). That is a slogan that will still work for us today.

Eucharistic divisions

The Eucharist ought to be a setting where our unity as Church is dramatically expressed; but, as we all know, sometimes the reverse is the case. This can be either because this particular community is divided (and such a thing does happen in Christian churches, as you will be aware), or because one denomination is divided from another, and does not practise Eucharistic hospitality towards them. My own Catholic tradition offers the Eucharist only to Orthodox churches, for reasons that at a certain period made good sense (though Orthodox churches do not reciprocate, on the grounds that our orders are not valid), while Anglicans offer Eucharistic hospitality to virtually all Christians. There were probably good reasons for these excommunications; but it may be that the time has come to reconsider them.

The problem as it presents itself in the Corinthian church, however, is of a different order. This is how Paul describes it (11:17-22):

> I do not praise you, because when you come together it is for the worse, not for the better. For in the first place, I hear that when you come together as an assembly[55] there are divisions[56] among you . . . so when you come together it is not to eat the Lord's Supper.[57] For each of you has their own supper in advance: and some people go hungry, while others are drunk! Don't you have homes for eating and drinking in? Do you despise the Church of God, and put to shame the have-nots?

Then (eyes on Christ once more, you see) he reminds them of the tradition that he had passed down to them about the Last Supper (11:23-5):

> For I received from the Lord, what I also passed on to you,
> that the Lord Jesus,
> on the night when he was being betrayed,
> took bread, and having given thanks, broke it and said,
> 'This is my body, which is for you.
> Do it for my memorial.'
> And likewise the cup, after supper, saying,
> 'This cup is the new covenant in my blood.
> Do this, as often as you drink it, for my memorial.'

---

55. This is a possible translation of the Greek word *ekklesia*, which could also be rendered as 'church'.
56. *Schismata* again.
57. You will have to imagine what kind of a shock the Corinthians will have received when this sentence was read out to them.

The argument comes to its end, after a firm reminder about the death of Jesus, with a practical injunction for coping with division at the Eucharist (vv.33, 34):

> So, my brothers and sisters, when you come together to eat, wait for each other. If someone is ravenous, let him or her eat at home!

The 'hymn to love'

At this point, Paul touches on another source of division in Corinth, namely their spiritual gifts; and now he uses the metaphor of the body, which we mentioned above.[58] Then he makes his last despairing attempt in this letter to get them to 'sing from the same hymn-sheet', in the great song to love, that you hear (quite properly) at practically every wedding you attend. You will find it at chapter 13, but notice how Paul introduces it, at 12:31: 'look for the superior gifts – and I am showing you a way that is very much better'.

Here is perhaps the prime example in Paul of 'keeping one's eyes on Christ' as a way of coping with division. For what Paul does, and alas it looks, as we shall see, as though it did not work, is to paint a picture of how love works, and if you look carefully you will see that it is a portrait of his beloved Jesus. In the first three verses, Paul emphasises the uselessness of various admirable religious practices, unless they are underpinned by love: speaking in tongues, prophecy and knowledge of mysteries, knowledge, faith so as to move mountains, and giving away possessions.

Then he draws the portrait of love ('eyes on Jesus'). Try reading this as a description of Jesus, and then, as an examination of conscience, reading it as a description of the Corinthian Christians, or even of yourself (13:4-8):

> Love is patient,
> love is kindly,[59]
> is not jealous,
> does not behave arrogantly,
> is not 'puffed up',
> does not behave indecently,
> does not seek its own,
> does not get irritated,
> does not keep a list of evils,
> does not rejoice in injustice – but rejoices in the truth.
> Love bears everything, believes everything,
> hopes for everything, endures everything.
> Love never fails.

---

58. See pp.45-7.
59. In Greek, this would have sounded like 'is Christly'.

Then Paul returns to the Corinthians and their defects, on which they so prided themselves (v.8):

> As for prophecies, they shall be abrogated.
> As for tongues, they shall stop.
> As for knowledge, it will be cancelled out.

After that, he offers what might look like autobiography but in fact continues the attack on the Corinthians, before the hymn reaches its climax (13:9-13):

> You see, we know [only] in part, and we prophesy [only] in part,
> but when the perfect comes that which is partial will be cancelled out.
> When I was an infant, I used to talk like an infant,
> I used to think like an infant,
> I used to count like an infant.
> But when I became an adult I cancelled out infant things.
> For just now we see through a mirror, in a riddle, but then face to face.
> Now I know in part, but then I shall know exactly as I am known.
> And so there remain: faith, hope, love, these three;
> and the greatest of these is love.

This is a powerful piece of writing, aimed directly into the Corinthian situation, but also one to bear in mind when we confront our own divisions.

Liturgical divisions

You cannot always tell how Paul is intending to structure his writing, but it must be said that this chapter 13 seems slightly to interrupt the flow from the end of chapter 12 to the beginning of 14. At all events, what we have in chapter 14 is Paul's treatment of liturgical confusion. In this case, it appears that the Corinthian charism of 'speaking in tongues' (on which they evidently prided themselves) was causing liturgical chaos. In his response, Paul suggests that prophecy and interpretation are to be preferred to tongues, because they communicate, and the whole purpose of liturgy should be 'that the Church may receive up-building' (14:5). That idea is repeated at 14:12: 'since you are seeking the spirits, seek [them] for the up-building of the church, that you may overflow [with gifts]'. Then he gives examples of liturgical behaviour that counts as building up the community (14:13-17):

> So the person speaking in a tongue should pray to give the interpretation:
> if I pray in a tongue, my spirit prays, but my mind does not bear fruit. So
> what are we to do? I'll pray in the Spirit, but I shall also pray in the mind;

I shall sing a song in the Spirit, but I shall also sing in the mind. You see, if you make a blessing in the Spirit, how is the one who performs the role of the outsider going to utter the 'Amen'? Because he has no idea what you are saying. For you are making a nice thanksgiving, but the other person is not built up.

Once again we meet the idea of up-building, and Paul reminds them that he is not exactly an amateur (14:18-20):

Thank God, I speak in tongues more than any of you, but in the church I prefer to speak five words with my mind, in order to instruct others, than ten thousand words in a tongue. Brothers and sisters, don't be children in your mindset. No – I want you to be infants with regard to evil, and perfect as regards your mindset.

Then Paul spells out the practical implications (14:27-33):

if someone speaks in a tongue, let them be two, or three at the most, and one after the other; and let one person give the translation. And if someone who is sitting down is given a revelation, let the first person sit down. For you can all prophesy one by one, so that all may learn something, and all get consoled . . . For God is not a God of disorder but of peace.

We do not know the precise situation with which Paul was dealing, but liturgy is often a divisive place, and the general tenor of Paul's remarks may be applicable to our contemporary divisions in that region.

Disagreement about resurrection

The next divisive issue is (as it might be in many places today) the question of what happens after death. You will find the question dealt with in chapter 15, where we are almost at the end of the letter. Some scholars see this as almost an afterthought, though others (and most of the time I count myself among them) regard this chapter as the climax of the letter.

Paul begins by reminding them of the terms in which he had preached the gospel, and that the gospel is nothing unless it is true about the resurrection of Jesus, to which Paul lists a series of reliable witnesses, including himself. That, however, is not really where the divisions lie; the problem seems to be that some members of the Corinthian church have died, and the question then is: are they lost forever, given that they have died before Jesus' return, or is there hope for them?

These arguments can speak to our situation, given that two thousand years later we are more inclined to expect to die than to look forward to Jesus' return in our lifetime. Paul's argument runs as follows:

- 15:1-11: Jesus was raised from the dead (as we told you when we first preached the gospel to you).

- 12-19: Therefore you who say there is no such thing as resurrection are wrong; and the answer is that you must keep your eyes on the Risen Christ.

- 20-28: The resurrection of everybody belongs with that of Christ.

- 29: What about people who are being baptised for the dead? [Here we should be cautious about assessing the argument, since we really do not know what Paul was talking about, though the Corinthians will certainly have known.]

- 30-34: This makes sense of the way Paul lives, but also means that the Corinthians must get their act together.

- 35-39: A possible objection: 'What kind of body will the risen dead receive?' The risen body will be different but appropriate. Think of the first and the second Adam. [If this argument does not seem easy to understand, probably the Corinthians will have grasped it; as it stands, it is rather abbreviated, and we are certainly struggling to make sense of it.]

Final thoughts

There are just three short passages that we should consider as Paul grapples with the divisions in Corinth.

The first is a startling piece of testimony for how serious the divisions were. It reads like this (16:1-4):

As for the collection for the saints:[60] as I commanded the churches of Galatia,[61] you are to do just the same.
On the first day of the week, each of you is to put [something] aside,[62] saving up anything where they have done well, so that when I come, then accounts can be drawn up. But when I come, the people whom you consider qualified, I am going to send them[63] with letters of accreditation, to carry your gift to Jerusalem. But if it is appropriate for me to go too,[64] they are to travel with me.

---

60. This is the collection for the impoverished Christians in Jerusalem, a cause dear to Paul's heart.
61. Paul does not want to single out the Corinthians for their meanness.
62. This may be significant: normally you would expect them to bring the money to church each Sunday; it looks as though the Corinthians did not trust each other not to steal it.
63. And they clearly do not trust Paul, either; he thinks that they will be reluctant for him to accompany the sending of the money.
64. Which is what Paul would clearly most like.

This is a rather sad, defeated ending to the letter.

Next comes another piece of evidence, the list of those who offer greetings across the sea (16:19-21):

> The churches of Asia greet you. Aquila and Priscilla greet you many times over in the Lord, along with the church in their house. All the brothers and sisters greet you. I want you to greet each other with a holy kiss. *The greeting in my hand: PAUL*

In the light of the evidence we have seen for the divisions in this church, we can understand the slightly desperate tone here. First we hear, not for the first time, of that partnership of Aquila and Priscilla; and the Corinthians are supposed to be impressed by the warmth of their greetings, and those of 'all the brothers and sisters'. Then, perhaps a bit nervously, Paul wants them to 'greet each other with a holy kiss' (something they will not have readily offered each other, but certainly needed, given their divisions). Finally, Paul snatches the pen from his secretary (he would normally dictate his letter) and adds his greetings and his signature, a reminder that he has had personal contact with the letter, and that they had better sort things out.

Finally, Paul reminds them of what is the vital thing (16:22, 23):

> If anyone does not love the Lord, let them be accursed.
> Maranatha.[65]
> My love be with all of you in Christ Jesus.

This is the answer to all our divisions: love the Lord Jesus, remember that Jesus is on his way (or perhaps already present); and love each other – in Christ Jesus.

So the letter to a very divided community comes to its end; we have squeezed it of all the available evidence, and can therefore treat the remaining two Pauline letters more briefly.

2 Corinthians – a painful history

You will not be surprised to learn that the divisions that we detected everywhere in 1 Corinthians are still visible in its successor. Indeed, Paul is so angry with them that, as in Galatians, he does not offer the conventional thanksgiving for their virtue. There is real tension between at least some of the Corinthian church and their founder.

---

65. An Aramaic, and therefore presumably early, formula, meaning either 'Come Lord', or 'the Lord has come', depending on how you space the syllables.

In the first place, there are accusations that Paul has been fickle in not coming to them. For at the end of the preceding letter, he had promised to come to them (1 Corinthians 16:5-7):

> I shall come to you when I go through Macedonia; for I am going through Macedonia, and perhaps I shall stay with you, or even spend the winter with you . . . for I have no desire to see you at the moment in passing. For I am hoping to spend some time with you, if the Lord permits.

However, he has not turned up, and we listen to the consequences (2 Corinthians 1:15-19):

> I was intending to come to you earlier, for you to get a double gift, and then to go through you by way of Macedonia, and again, after Macedonia, to come back . . . When I was intending this, was I going in for fickleness? Or was I intending in a non-spiritual way, that it should be 'Yes, Yes' and 'No, no' with me? God is reliable: our word to you is not 'Yes and No'. For the Son of God, Jesus Christ who was proclaimed among you through us, that is through me and Silvanus and Timothy was not 'Yes and No'. On the contrary: 'Yes' has come to be in him.

You can feel in these verses the accusations that they have been laying against him: 'Paul doesn't mean a word he says.' But notice what is Paul's answer to them, and it is already familiar to us as the way of coping with divisions in the early Church (and in ours): keep your eyes on God and on Christ.

Not only that, but we have a good deal of autobiography in this letter, and, as I said before with regard to Galatians, we must always be grateful to the people who annoy Paul, because he only tells us anything about himself when he gets cross. So we listen as he tells us why he did not come (1:23, 24):

> I call on God as my witness, on my life, that it was to spare you that I no longer came to Corinth! Not that we lord it over your faith. No – we are working together for your joy. For you stand firm in the faith.

We learn that there has been tension between them, and both sides were feeling the pain (2:1-4):

> For I decided in myself not to come back to you in pain. For if I cause you pain, then who is the person to cheer me up, except the person who was caused pain by me? And I wrote that very thing, so as not to come and receive pain from the very people who should have made me glad. I was confident in all of you that my joy consists of all of you. For it was out of

much affliction and distress of heart that I wrote to you, through many tears, not for you to be pained, but for you to know the overflowing love that I have for you.

The pain here is unmistakable, but then so also is the love that Paul has for his Corinthians; and that love, on top of the slogan 'eyes on God', may be the way modelled for dealing with our own divisions. We do not know quite what the letter was that he wrote; presumably it was not 1 Corinthians, and probably not the letter he refers to at 1 Corinthians 5:9, which seems to have been about 'having anything to do with those who are sexually immoral'. He says a bit more about it in chapter 7:

> Because even if I caused you pain with the letter, I am not sorry for it; and even if I was sorry for it, I see that that letter, even if it did cause you pain for a bit, now I am glad, not because you felt the pain, but because the pain made you turn it around . . . So if I did write to you, it was not because of the one who had done wrong, nor because of the one to whom wrong was done, but that your devotion for us might be made clear to you in God's presence.[66]

So there is pain in the relationship, and they have managed to sort it out (though, as we shall see, there is more to come); for our purposes, what is of interest is to see the techniques employed by Paul to deal with the divisions, namely a recognition of their mutual love, and keeping their eyes on God and on Christ Jesus.

We are, as is often said with regard to the Pauline letters, listening to just one side of the telephone conversation: the Corinthians knew what he was talking about, and we do not. However, one thing is clear – that there has been criticism of him in Corinth (10:1, 2):

> I, Paul, am begging you, through the meekness and graciousness of Christ, I who am 'in person humble among you, but when I am away I am very brave in your regard'.[67] I am begging you not [to have] to be brave with that self-confidence with which I reckon to be daring against some people who think of me as walking in the flesh.

Again it is hard for us to know precisely what was going on, though the Corinthians will certainly have got it. But they have been saying unpleasant things about him (10:9-11):

---

66. 7: 8, 9, 12. If the translation seems unduly clumsy, then blame Paul, not the translator.
67. Here, presumably, we can hear an accusation that the Corinthians have made against him. Notice the appeal to Christ, once more.

I don't want to seem to be trying to frighten you through the letters. 'He says his letters are weighty and strong; but his physical presence is unimpressive, and his rhetoric is not worth bothering about.' A person like this needs to take it into account that we are just the same in our rhetoric as we are in our letters when we are away and in what we do when we are present.

Here we are presumably eavesdropping on Paul's critics, which is a rare privilege. One of the things that has evidently been going on is that they have been comparing Paul unfavourably to some characters whom he refers to as 'the super-apostles' (11:5-11):

> For I reckon that I have not fallen short of the 'super-apostles'. Even if I am a 'non-specialist in rhetoric', I am a specialist in 'knowledge'. No – I have made it clear to you in every respect. Did I commit a sin when I humbled myself, so that you people might be exalted? (Because I gospelled the gospel of God to you for free.) I pillaged other churches and took payment [from them] in order to serve you! And when I came to you, and was short, I did not burden anybody. For the Christians who came from Macedonia supplied what I was lacking, and in every respect I kept myself from burdening you; and I shall continue to do so . . . Why? Because I don't love you? God knows [that I do].

We should love to know a bit more about this, but we can guess at the divisions that arouse such bitterness in him (even though by the end he admits to loving them).

Later on, and again because they have annoyed him, Paul goes on for more of what he calls 'boasting', though it is more about how much he has suffered than about the marvels he has performed, and he concludes, with bitter sarcasm (12:11-13):

> I have been a fool – and you forced me into it! I should have been recommended by you. For I am no way inferior to the 'super-apostles', even if I am 'nothing'. The 'apostle-signs' were performed among you with all steadfastness, with signs and wonders and miracles. For in what respect were you worse off than the rest of the churches, except that I myself did not burden you? Forgive me this injustice!!

Paul is very cross here, and it is hard to see how the divisions can be healed. Perhaps they never were. Listen to the last words of the extant Corinthian correspondence. You know it well, but may not always pick up the despair here (13:14):

> The grace of the Lord Jesus Christ, and the love of God and the solidarity of the Holy Spirit be with you all.

It sounds like just any old concluding greeting, but we might reflect how once more Paul is begging them to cope with their divisions by keeping their eyes on God and Christ, but that there is a shortage of 'grace' (God's free gift, remember) among them, and precious little love or solidarity. So these words may be shot through with pain, especially since, half a century later, Clement Bishop of Rome is still writing to the same Corinthian church, begging them to put an end to their divisions. We Christians are sometimes addicted to what divides us.

Romans – an exercise in diplomacy, a church that Paul had not founded

If you listen carefully to the Letter to the Romans, you can hear the sound of Paul treading gently on eggshells. The church in Rome had not been founded by Paul (or Peter, come to that); we do not know how the message about Jesus had reached Rome, but there had been for a long time a good number of Jews in Rome; and very likely it was quite soon that some of them were starting to announce their belief that Jesus was the Messiah. This may have led to tension, and certainly we know from the Roman historian Suetonius that in AD49 the Emperor Claudius had decreed something against them, probably not, as Suetonius supposed, that *all* Jews were expelled, but only those who were followers of Jesus, since he seems to refer to an *agent provocateur* called 'Chrestus'. A likely story is that when the expelled group returned to Rome after Claudius' death, they found that Gentile Christians were now in charge, and that therefore one of the sources of the tension that we can detect reading between the lines of the letter would be Gentile–Jewish rivalry, a struggle for power in the Church. Paul has to go very delicately.

Another reason for this may also be the intemperate language that he had used in the letter to the Galatians, especially with regard to some of the Jewish Christians who had come from Jerusalem. There seem to have been links between the Jerusalem community and the Jewish Christians in Rome, so one possibility is that Paul was aware that his name was known, and not especially highly regarded, in Rome, and that his letter to this hitherto unvisited church was meant to address the problem.

Winning the Romans over

This may be why he goes to such lengths to win over their goodwill, speaking (1:8) of the extent to which the faith of the Roman Christians is known 'in the whole world', and of 'how unceasingly I make remembrance of you always, asking in my prayers that I may do well enough, by God's will. For I am longing to see you, that I may share some spiritual free gift, for you to be strengthened' (1:9-11). Then he remembers that he cannot represent himself as just bringing them something: 'that is to say, to find joint comfort among you, because of the faith that we find in each other, your faith and mine' (1:12). Then, in case they start to complain that he has been a bit slow to make it to Rome, he says (1:13): 'I do not want you to be unaware, brothers and sisters, that it was frequently my plan to come to you (but I was prevented up to the present moment) in order to gain some fruit, among you as well as among the rest of the Gentiles.' Then he offers what some scholars (possibly overstating matters by a fraction) regard as a summary of the entire letter (1:16):

> You see, I am not afraid of the gospel. For it is the power of God, for salvation to everyone who comes to faith, first Jew and then non-Jew.

Notice that emphasis on the priority of Jews over 'non-Jews' ('nations' or 'Gentiles' in Paul's Greek), a pointer to the delicacy of the situation. He repeats this phrase at 2:9, and comes back to the question in the all-important section, chapters 9–11, where he deals with the question, which was no doubt a pressing one in that mixed Roman church, about Paul's fellow Jews – what was God's plan for them?

Lulling them into complacency

So in chapter 1, we can hear the Jewish Christian listeners cheering as Paul lays into the Gentiles (1:28-32):

> And because they did not think it worthwhile to come to acknowledge God, God handed them over to an unworthwhile[68] state of mind, doing things that ought not to be done, filled with every kind of immorality, wickedness, greed, badness, overloaded with envy, murder,[69] strife, trickery, malice, slander; they talk people down, they hate God, they are arrogant and overweening boasters, inventors of vices, disobedient to their parents,[70] uncomprehending, untrustworthy, unfeeling, unmerciful. Although they recognise God's commandment, that people who do things like this are worthy of death, not only do they do them, they actually approve of those who act this way.

---

68. This invented term is an attempt to catch Paul's wordplay in this verse.
69. 'Envy' and 'murder' will have sounded very similar as the text was read out in the Roman church.
70. This may seem a fairly mild form of sin, but Paul's Jewish listeners will have been aware that 'honour your father and mother' was the first of the ten commandments to deal with relations with other human beings.

Then, just as they cry, 'Yes, Paul: tell them how it is!', he now turns on his Jewish hearers (2:1; 17-24):

> So you have no defence, any of you who condemn; for in so far as you condemn the other person, you pass sentence on yourself, for you who condemn do just the same yourself!
>
> If you, who call yourself a Jew, and find your comfort in the Law, and boast of God, and if you know [God's] will, and you approve the things that really matter, because you have been instructed from the Law, and you are confident of being a guide for the blind, a light for those in darkness, an educator of the mindless, a teacher of infants, since you have the proper shape of knowledge and of truth, because of the Law, if you who teach the other person fail to teach yourself, you proclaim 'Thou shalt not steal', and actually steal, and you say 'Thou shalt not commit adultery', and actually commit adultery, and you who detest idols actually rob temples, you who boast of the Law, dishonour God by transgressing the Law. Because, as it is written, God's name is blasphemed through you among the Gentiles.

This is very strong language, and we mop our brow as we read it. The point of the argument is that everyone, Jews and non-Jews, need what God has done in Christ.

What about the Jews?

For our purposes, looking for evidence of divisions in the early Church and how they solved them, that is enough, and we need not at this point follow the difficult argumentation that Paul now elaborates. Instead we can jump directly to chapter 9, and we must have no doubt that Paul longs for Jews to hear the word, and to hold out a hand of friendship to those fellow Jews of his who do not believe that the Messiah has come (9:1-5):

> I am telling the truth in Christ; I am not lying, and my conscience is witnessing in my defence: there is an enormous pain and an unceasing sorrow in my heart. For I (I, myself!) prayed to be accursed from Christ on behalf of my brothers and sisters, my [Jewish] kinsfolk according to the flesh.
>
> They are Israelites;
> theirs is the adoption-as-sons, and the glory,
> and the covenants and the lawgiving and the divine worship, and the promises.
> Theirs are the patriarchs, and from them came Christ in the flesh.
> May the God who is above all be blessed forever.[71] Amen!

---

71. Or: 'Christ in the flesh, God over all, blessed forever'. This would be a very strong statement of the divinity of Christ, but it is certainly a possible reading of the text.

There is no mistaking the pain here in Paul's voice; one of the very biggest issues of that first century was: what about the Jews? This question arose in two ways: first, why has a Jewish reform movement not attracted more Jews, given that Jesus and all his first disciples were Jews and were devotees of the Jewish God, while, on the other hand, vast numbers of non-Jews came flooding in? Secondly, what should the infant Church ask of these non-Jews (known as 'Greeks' or 'Gentiles') who came into the movement? Did they have to be circumcised and observe the Sabbath and Jewish dietary laws? We are witnesses here to a point of painful division, and to Paul's determination to overcome the division.

The body once more

So Paul comes back to his image of 'the body'. We have already seen this image at work in Colossians and Ephesians, and how Paul used it precisely to deal with divisions. Here, once more, he is using it in the context of the painful divisions in the Roman church (12:1-8):

And so I am begging you, brothers and sisters, through the compassion of God, to offer your bodies as a living and holy sacrifice, pleasing to God, your reasonable sacrifice [the alert reader will here observe that Paul is using the language of Jewish worship, and this may reflect precisely the tension between Jews and Gentiles in the Roman church] . . .

. . . for just as in one body, we have many parts,[72] but not all the parts have the same function, so we who are many are one body in Christ, and individually parts of each other, having different charisms in accordance with the grace that has been given us,

whether prophecy, according to the proportion of faith,
or service, in serving-at-table,
or teaching, in teaching lessons,
or giving comfort, in comforting,
or sharing, in generosity,
or in giving leadership, in devotion,
or giving mercy, cheerfully.

You can see here how Paul is trying to mitigate the pains of division in the Roman church, and how the idea of the body operates in a slightly different way. Is there something here for us to reflect on today?

---

72. Or 'limbs' or 'members'.

Should they pay tax to unjust governments?

Another potentially neuralgic issue is the question of paying taxes. It is quite likely that there were several views on this question in the Roman church, some thinking (like the author of the Book of Revelation) that Rome is such an evil power that we should never pay any taxes to it.[73] Others, including, I suspect, Paul himself, who according to Acts (16:35-9; 22:25-9) was proud of his Roman citizenship, and will no doubt have been well aware of how well-maintained roads, a good postal service, and a Mediterranean cleared of pirates helped him in preaching the gospel, took a different attitude. This may explain what he now writes (13:1-8):

> Let every soul be subordinated to the superior authorities.
> For all authority is under God, and those that exist are appointed by God.
> So the one who resists authority is opposed to God's ordinance;
> and those who are opposed will take condemnation on themselves.
> For rulers are not sources of terror for [those who do] a good work,
> but for [those who do] evil.
> Do you wish not to be afraid of authority?
> Do good, and you will get praise from it.
> For [authority] is God's servant for your good,
> a wrathful avenger for those who do evil.
> So it is necessary to be subordinated [to them],
> not just because of their anger, but also for conscience's sake.
> That is the reason for paying taxes;
> for they are God's servants, occupying themselves for that very service.
> Repay everyone what you owe,
> tribute to the tribute collector,
> taxes to the tax collector
> and reverence to those to whom you owe reverence,
> honour to those to whom you owe honour.
> Do not owe anyone anything except to love each other,
> for the one who loves has fulfilled the other Law.

You can see how at one and the same time Paul is dealing with a potentially painful question and insisting on the importance of love, and citing Jesus' teaching about the Law. That is still a lesson for us today, in dealing with our divisions.

---

73. A good friend of mine, who was a 'hermit in the city' in the far North West of the United States, had to earn a living, but made sure that she earned no more than the lowest tax limit, for she did not wish her money to be used in support of nuclear weapons.

What to do about differing sensitivities in the Church?

The fact is that in any organisation, including Christian churches, there are many different and deeply held attitudes. Paul offers some helpful suggestions, as valid today as for the church in Rome, on how to cope (14:1-3):

Be accepting of those who are weak in faith, so as not to have ideological disputes.

One person [for example] believes that [they can] eat anything; a weak person [only] eats vegetables.

[In that case] the person [who eats everything] is not to despise the person who does not.

And the person who does not eat everything is not to judge the one who does – for God has accepted that person.

What about vegans?

Dietary questions can arouse very strong passions in every culture, and what Paul is telling the Roman Christians is that, in the end, it does not matter all that much. We may need to remember that in our discussions across religious boundaries. And Catholicism in particular entails accepting diversity (more than Catholics sometimes realise). Absolutely central, of course, is having respect for fellow Christians. Paul makes that point later in the same chapter (14:13-21):

So let us not judge[74] one another. Let us instead make this our judgement: not to put an obstacle or a stumbling-block in the way of a brother or sister. I know and I am persuaded in the Lord Jesus that nothing is unclean in itself, but if because someone thinks it is unclean, that is what makes it so. Therefore, if your brother or sister is pained because of food, you are no longer behaving in a loving way. You are not, by what you eat, to destroy the one for whom Christ died. Don't let your good be the subject of blasphemy. For the Kingdom of God is not a matter of what we eat or drink, but of righteousness, and peace, and joy in the Holy Spirit. For the one who is a slave of Christ in this matter is pleasing to God, and esteemed by human beings. Therefore let us pursue the things that make for peace, and the things that build us up into each other. Don't undo God's work in the matter of food: everything is clean, but it can be bad for the person who

---

74. Or 'condemn'.

eats through creating an obstacle. It is good not to eat meat or drink wine, and not to do anything that creates an obstacle for your fellow Christian.

This is excellent advice for handling our divisions; not by ideology, but by consideration for one another. Once more, we notice, love is the criterion. This is what underlies our next text, what you might call a 'warning to the "strong"' (15:1, 2):

> We who are powerful ought to carry the weaknesses of those who are powerful, and not please ourselves. Let each of us please our neighbour, aiming at the good, to *build up*.

Once again we see how Paul insists on the notion of 'up-building' as a criterion for our behaviour.

Names to conjure with

There is something of this in the final chapter, when Paul gives the Romans a list of names (remember that he is aware that he is not necessarily addressing a sympathetic audience here) of people who can vouch for him, though ostensibly he is simply greeting those people (16:1-16):

> I am commending our sister Phoebe to you, who is the deacon of the church at Cenchreae. I want you to give her hospitality in the Lord, in a manner that is worthy of the saints, and to be at her disposal for whatever she needs; for she has been a protector of many people, including myself.
>
> I want you to greet Prisca and Aquila, my fellow workers in Christ Jesus, who risked their necks for my life, and it is not just I who thank them, but all the churches of the Gentiles, and I want you to greet the church that is in their house.
>
> I want you to greet Epainetus, my beloved, who is the first fruits of Asia for Christ.
>
> Give greetings to Maria, who has done much work for you.
>
> Give greetings to Andronicus and Junia, my fellow Jews and fellow prisoners, who are conspicuous among the apostles, who were ahead of me in Christ.
>
> Give greetings to Ampliatus my beloved in the Lord.

Give greetings to Urbanus, my fellow worker in Christ, and Stachys my beloved.

Give greetings to Apelles, who has stood the test in Christ.

Give greetings to those who are from Aristoboulos' lot.

Give greetings to Herodion, my fellow Jew; give greetings to those who are from Narcissus' lot, those who are in the Lord.

Greet Tryphaena and Tryphosa, who laboured in the Lord.

Give my greetings to the beloved [lady] Persis; she has laboured much in the Lord.

Give greetings to Rufus, the chosen one in the Lord, and to his mother (and mine).

Give greetings to Asynkritos, Phlegon, Hermes, Patrobas, Hermas, and the brothers and sisters with them.

Give greetings to Philologos and Julia, Nereus and his sister, and Olympus and all the saints who are with them.

I want you to greet each other with a holy kiss. All the churches of Christ give you greetings.

What we should notice here is that Paul is dealing with real people with real needs, and in so doing he is giving us a model for how to handle our divisions. In part, it is true, he is helping his own cause, but he is also showing how Christians need to regard one another.

A word for 'division'

Finally in this letter, let us observe a word that means 'divisions'. The Greek is *dichostasia*, which is used in the New Testament only here and at Galatians 5:20, as part of Paul's list of the 'works of the flesh', and therefore something to be avoided at all costs (16:17, 18):

I am begging you, brothers and sisters, to watch out for people who create divisions and stumbling blocks, contrary to the teaching that you learned:

steer clear of them. You see, people like this are not servants of Christ our Lord, but of their own bellies; and through plausible speech and blessings they deceive the hearts of the unsuspecting.

This letter, Paul's greatest in many ways, has much to teach us about how to deal with our divisions, through love and through keeping our eyes on Christ.

CHAPTER 4

Handling divisions in Acts

Introduction

It is good to read Acts at this point, after looking at the letters attributed to and written by Paul, who dominates the story of Acts after chapter 13. This remarkable text, the second volume of Luke's Gospel (which we shall be reading in a later chapter, to see what it tells us about divisions) indicates that divisions happen, even in the early Church. It also serves to remind us that the Holy Spirit is capable of working through our divisions to quite unexpected results. God can cope even with our divisions.

These fractures are evident from quite early on in Acts; one example between Jesus and his disciples occurs just before the moment of the Ascension, when these dimwits brightly ask him, 'Lord – is it at this time that you are restoring the kingdom to Israel?' (1:6), which indicates that they have not been listening to a word he has said to them.

Those same disciples are reprimanded by angels for looking in the wrong direction: 'Why are you standing, gazing at the sky?' (1:11).

Then there is a reminder of another kind of division, as Peter asks them what to do about replacing Judas, and Matthias is ordained by lot; at which point he disappears, never to be heard of again (1:15-26). This is a reminder that those who are called can abandon Jesus, as Judas did; however, we also learn that God can cope whatever we do.

Contrasting pictures in Acts

Luke is a remarkable artist, and can paint a picture with just a few strokes of his pen. A good example of this is to be found in his deftly drawn 'summaries', which, especially in the first seven chapters of Acts, paint a picture of undivided unity and pleasant harmony in the early Church. This was a technique that Luke will have found in Mark's Gospel, but which he greatly elaborated. Consider this passage (2:42-7):

> They were persevering in the teaching of the apostles, and in solidarity, in the breaking of the bread[75] and in prayers. And there came awe on every soul, and many signs and wonders came to be through the apostles.

---

75. Presumably the Eucharist.

All those who believed were on the same mission; and they held everything in common. They would sell possessions and properties, and divide them amongst everybody according as someone had need. Every day they were persevering unanimously in the Temple, and they broke bread at home; they shared food with gladness[76] and generosity of heart. They would praise God; and they had favour with the entire people. And the Lord was adding every day to the number of those who were being saved, to the same end.

It is a lovely picture, and we should rejoice in it, and recognise that Christians have tried to live that way ever since, even if we do not always manage it. Luke does the same again two chapters later (4:32-5):

There was one heart and one mind in the crowd of those who had come to faith; and not one of them would claim that any of their possessions was their own. They held everything in common.

And with great power, the apostles used to give witness to the Resurrection of the Lord Jesus; and there was great grace[77] upon all of them. For there was no one in need among them. For anyone who owned estates or houses sold them; and they would bring the price of what they had sold, and lay them at the feet of the apostles. And it was distributed to each one according as anyone had need.

Now a picture like that can make us feel depressed that in our day we do not do better in building Christian community; but in the very next episode, Luke cheers us up by allowing us to glimpse that life in the early Church was not always quite so inspiring (5:1-11):

Now there was a man named Ananias, with his wife Sapphira, who sold a possession. He kept back part of the price, with his wife's consent; and brought a part of it, which he put at the feet of the apostles. Now Peter said, 'Ananias – why did Satan fill your heart for you to cheat the Holy Spirit and keep back some of the price of the land? If it had remained with you, would it not have remained? And when it was sold, did it not remain under your authority? Why did you put this business into your heart? It was not human beings whom you cheated, but God.' When Ananias heard these words, he fell down and expired. And there came awe on all those who heard of it. And the younger men got up and removed him, took him out and buried him.

---

76. Continuing Jesus' habit of banquets that expressed his practice of solidarity with the marginalised.
77. Or 'favour'.

Now there was an interval of about three hours and his wife, who did not know what had happened, came in. Peter said to her, 'Tell me – was it for such-and-such a price that you sold the land?' She said, 'Yes, such-and-such.' Peter said to her, 'Why did [the two of] you conspire to tempt the Spirit of the Lord? Look! The feet of those who have buried your husband are at the door, and they are going to carry you out.'

Immediately she fell down and expired. The young men came in and found her dead. And they carried her out and buried her next to her husband. And great awe came on the entire church, and on all who heard this.

People get very worried about this story, and endeavour to defend Peter against the charge of murder; but I should like to suggest to you that the tale does not take itself altogether seriously, but uses the story to indicate, immediately after the previous summary, which it echoes in places, that not everything in the early Church was as harmonious as you might think. When we are tempted to cheat the community, we are acting against what is best in us, which is already a kind of death. The contrast between these two pictures can tell us a great deal.

Divisions that lead to death

Another interesting picture that Luke paints, illustrative of divisions in the early Church, and their unexpected effects, is the long story that starts with an outbreak of racial hostility in chapter 6, leads in the end to death, and then, unexpectedly, to the successful preaching of the gospel. We start with the account of racial and religious tension (6:1-5):

In these days, when the disciples were multiplying, there arose a grumbling on the part of the Greek speakers against the Hebrew speakers, on the grounds that their widows were being overlooked in the daily distribution.

And the Twelve summoned the crowd of disciples, and said, 'It is not desirable for us to abandon the word of God and serve at tables. So, brothers [and sisters], choose seven men from among you who have a good reputation, full of the Holy Spirit and of wisdom, whom we shall put in charge for this necessity. We shall devote ourselves to prayer and to the service of the word.' This suggestion was acceptable to the whole community,[78] and they chose:

---

78. Or 'crowd'.

Stephen, a man full of faith and of the Holy Spirit,
and Philip,
and Prochorus
and Nicanor
and Timon
and Parmenas
and Nicolaos, a proselyte from Antioch.

We should notice two things here: first, that all seven of these have good Greek names, and that Nicolaos hails from the multi-racial city of Antioch; and, second, that we only hear of two of them again, namely Stephen and Philip; and neither of them will be waiting at table when we do. The Spirit has enterprising ways of dealing with our divisions.

The next thing that happens is that Stephen, 'full of grace and power', goes in for a highly successful, if all too brief, career of 'signs and wonders'. This brings him into opposition with

some people from the synagogue known as 'Of the Libertines', and from the Cyreneans, and Alexandrians and of those from Cilicia and Asia, arguing with Stephen (6:9).

However (6:10-14):

they were unable to resist the wisdom and spirit[79] with which he was speaking. Then they secretly produced some men who said, 'We heard him speaking blasphemous words against Moses and God.' They caused agitation among the people and the elders and scribes, and they set on him and dragged him off and took him to the Sanhedrin, and they set up false witnesses who said 'This fellow never stops speaking words against this holy Place[80] and against the Torah. Because we heard him saying that this fellow Jesus the Nazarene is going to destroy this Place, and corrupt the morals that Moses handed down to us.'

In response, Stephen delivers a highly subversive speech for the defence at his trial (7:2-53), which leads to his conviction and death (7:54–8:1), which was not precisely what we had in mind when we read about his being appointed to 'serve at table'. However, the story has a great deal more life in it, first because we are introduced to a young man called Saul who looked after the clothes of

---

79. Or 'Spirit'.
80. The word 'place' is a regular euphemism for the Temple in Jewish writing, so I have capitalised the word here.

Stephen's executioners (7:58), and 'was consenting to his destruction' (8:1),[81] and secondly because another chain of events then starts, so that what looks like a tragedy turns into an unexpected success.

This is how it goes: the people of God are 'scattered'[82] through the regions of Judea and Samaria (8:2). This echoes 1:8, where Jesus had said, 'You are to be my witnesses in Jerusalem and all Judaea and Samaria and to the ends of the earth'; this command outlines the programme that we see developing through the rest of Acts, the Spirit working despite all divisions. Now we read that 'Paul was ravaging the church, going into house after house, and dragging off men and women and handing them over into gaol' (8:3).

It sounds as though these inner Jewish disagreements spell disaster for the infant Jesus movement; but in fact this leads to the gospel reaching Africa, in the shape of the following story, where the hero is the second of the Greek-speaking males appointed to 'serve at table', namely Philip (8:26-30):

> The angel of the Lord spoke to Philip,[83] saying, 'Up you get, and journey to the South, on the road that goes down from Jerusalem to Gaza' [this is desert]. And he got up and journeyed. And look! An Ethiopian man, a eunuch, a potentate of the Kandake, the Queen of the Ethiopians, who was in charge of all her Treasury. He had gone up to worship in Jerusalem; and he was coming back and sitting on his chariot, and was reading the prophet Isaiah. And the Spirit said to Philip, 'Approach and stick to this chariot.' So Philip ran up to him, and heard him reading Isaiah, and said, 'Do you know what you are reading?'

The upshot of this story (and remember that it all started with racial tensions in the Church) is that, after appropriate instruction from Philip, the eunuch is baptised as they pass by some water. After that the Spirit intervenes (for the third time):

> The Spirit snatched Philip up, and the eunuch did not see him any more, for he was journeying on his road rejoicing (8:39).

From there the gospel, in the form of Philip, reaches Caesarea (8:40), where we shall later (21:8, 9) meet Philip once more, along with his four prophesying daughters.

So the consequences of that division between those who spoke Aramaic and those who spoke Greek have been, literally, far reaching. And there is

---

81. The alert reader is well aware that we shall hear more of this young man.
82. A word that we shall be hearing again.
83. Whom we can therefore acquit of disobedience in the matter.

more; for earlier on, we made reference to the word 'scattering', and the effect that this consequence of the death of Stephen had on the gospel. Now it has a further effect; for at 11:19, we read of 'those who had been scattered as a result of the trouble that happened because of Stephen', and it turns out that, precisely because of this 'scattering', the gospel reaches Cyprus, the nearest large island to Palestine in the Mediterranean, Antioch, presumably the great city in Syria, and Cyrene, which is in Africa (reminding us of the spectacular spread depicted under the influence of the Holy Spirit on the feast of Pentecost, back at 2:9-11). Then it reaches the Greeks, where all the trouble had started (11:20):

> And some of them [those who had been *scattered* – 11:19] were men from Cyprus and Cyrene, who had come to Antioch and started talking also to Greek speakers,[84] giving the good news of the Lord Jesus.

You see the pattern: precisely as a result of the tensions, and of the death of Stephen, the gospel has been spread to an unimaginable range of people. So the Holy Spirit can cope with all our divisions and the Church can actually profit by them.

We shall soon be looking at another set of divisions that arose in consequence, with angry accusations of a lack of orthodoxy.

Back to the young man called Saul

For the moment, we go back to the story of the death of Stephen; for you will recall that we saw there a young man called Saul. He now reappears very rapidly, at 9:1, 2. This is the story, told in narrative form (he tells it twice more in Acts – in autobiographical mode to his fellow Jews at 22:1-21, and to King Agrippa at 26:1-23) in the third person, of how he encountered Jesus. For our purposes, the interest lies in the fact that the young man's change of heart does not create an immediate welcome in the Christian community. Not surprisingly, they are very cautious about accepting Saul, and tensions clearly remain, as Ananias explains in his courteous response to the Lord's invitation to go and find Saul and lay (healing!) hands upon him (9:13, 14):

> Ananias answered, 'Lord – I have heard from many people about this man, what great evils he has done to your saints in Jerusalem; and here he is, with authority from the High Priests to arrest all those who call upon your name.'

---

84. This is the Greek word 'Hellenists'; here presumably it carries the notion of 'Gentiles', rather than 'Greek-speaking Jews'.

We see the same hesitation on the part of Christians with regard to Saul, later in the same chapter (9:26, 27):

> When he got to Jerusalem [Saul] tried to join the disciples; but they were all afraid of him, not convinced that he was a disciple. But Barnabas took him up and brought him to the apostles, and explained to them how [Saul] had seen the Lord on the way, and that he had spoken to him, and how [Saul] had been quite open in speaking in the name of Jesus.

So, bit by bit, the tensions are dissipated, and the divisions healed; and Luke provides one of his characteristic summaries, indicating that all is well (9:31):

> So the church in the whole of Judea and Galilee and Samaria was at peace, being built up and journeying in the fear of the Lord, and the comfort of the Holy Spirit; and it was on the increase.

Divisions are not therefore the end of the story; they are there, and will happen, but we can cope with them by keeping our eyes on God and on Jesus ('fear of the Lord', as Luke puts it).

Accusations of abandoning orthodox doctrine

You may be interested to learn that there were allegations that Peter and others were abandoning hallowed teaching. Indeed, you may feel that it has something of a contemporary ring. The issue in this case was about eating non-kosher food; and as you read the tale, you might think of what is the contemporary equivalent in the part of the world where you are reading these words.

The story starts in chapter 10, where the Holy Spirit brings together two people from very different backgrounds. The first of these is Cornelius, a centurion of the Italica cohort, and presumably a Gentile, though open to Jewish ways, as Luke tells us that he is 'devout and a God-fearer, along with all his household, doing much almsgiving and praying to God in every respect' (10:2). Once again, Luke creates atmosphere; with just a few phrases he has given us the picture. Then this pious Gentile is granted a vision (10:3-6):

> He clearly saw in a vision the angel of the Lord, about the ninth hour, coming into him, and addressing him, 'Cornelius ... your prayers and your almsgiving have gone up as a memorial offering before God. Now you are to send men to Joppa and summon a certain Simon, who is surnamed "Rock". This man is staying as a guest of one Simon the Tanner, who has a house by the sea.'

Cornelius obediently does what he is told, and we notice that God is in charge of events; so whatever is going to take place must be good. Now (10:9-15) the scene switches to the other partner in the dialogue, and on the next day, as Cornelius' messengers are on their way, Peter ('Rock')

> went up onto the roof to pray, at about the sixth hour. He became very hungry and wanted to taste something. While they were getting it ready, a trance seized him, and he sees heaven opened, and coming down a container of some kind, like a big sheet let down by its four corners. In it there were all the quadrupeds and creepy-crawlies of the earth, and the birds of the air. And there came a voice to him, 'Up you get, Peter, sacrifice and eat.' But Peter said, 'No way, Lord; because I never ate anything profane or unclean.'

> And again, a second time, a voice came to him, 'What God has declared clean, you are not to regard as profane.'

The tension is set up, and the narrative demands a resolution. Then, just as Peter is scratching his head about all this, Cornelius' messengers are knocking on the door, and the Spirit intervenes (10:19, 20):

> 'Look! There are three men looking for you. But up you get, and go down and travel with them without any hesitation; I have sent them.'

Then if we are reading attentively, we should be very startled, for as we watch we see that Peter, the good Jew, ends up by doing something that is really quite shocking (10:23):

> He invited them in and gave them hospitality.

His education continues, for he travels with them the next day, and arrives at Cornelius' house, where he has to discourage Cornelius from giving inappropriate homage ('Get up – I too am a human being'); notice how at every point he is treading on neuralgic points that could have caused immense divisions in that complex society. He is not daunted, however, but treats these very different people as equals (10:27, 28):

> He was chatting with them, went in, and found that many people had got together. He said to them, 'You people know that it is unlawful for a Jewish male to stick with or even to approach non-Jews. But God has shown me that I must not call any human being profane or unclean. That is why I came without making any objection when you sent for me.'

This could be a model for our dealings today with those who are of different cultures. In this instance, Peter's attitude enables the story (driven by the Holy Spirit) to reach its important conclusion at 10:44-48:

> While Peter was still uttering these words [to the effect that 'God is no snob' and that Jesus died for everybody], the Holy Spirit fell upon all those who were listening to the word. And the believers who were of the circumcision party, those who had come with Peter, were astounded: 'Even on the Gentiles the free gift of the Holy Spirit has been poured out.' For they heard them speaking in tongues, and magnifying God. And Peter responded, 'Surely nobody can withhold water for baptising these people? They have received the Holy Spirit, just like us.' He gave instructions for them to be baptised in the name of Jesus Christ. Then they asked him to stay for three days.

Peter's readiness to see what God is doing and saying has laid the ground for this remarkable conversion; and it should model our own behaviour in dealing with religious divisions. Notice, however, that there is still a problem, for Peter has done something that is not technically permissible, and might reasonably be classed as 'unorthodox'. So there are consequences, when Peter gets back to Jerusalem, for the story has been 'tweeted' around the Holy Land, for the church authorities (11:1-3)

> had heard that the Gentiles had accepted the word of God. And when Peter went up to Jerusalem, those of the circumcision party said, 'Why did you go in to men who have uncircumcision and eat with them?'

This is a familiar attitude in certain religious quarters, for at our worst we can find ourselves taking refuge in our rigidities about 'what the Law says'. The answer lies, as it always must, in what God has done, and that is the story that Peter now tells, at the end of which (11:18):

> When they had heard this, they kept their peace; and they glorified God, saying 'Indeed God has granted repentance-for-life to Gentiles also.'

So the tension is now dissolved. Here is surely a good model for handling our divisions today. Like our present neuralgic issues, however, the issue does not easily go away; for at 15:1 it arises again. This is the episode that is sometimes called the 'First Council of Jerusalem'; and a painful issue is resolved by some wise listening, a mode that the Church will do well to imitate today when dealing with such anguished topics. Reach for your New Testament, and see how it goes. The episode begins with the problem being outlined: Antioch is disturbed by visitors from Judaea insisting on circumcision; Paul and Barnabas (not surprisingly) resist, and the matter is referred to Jerusalem, where 'they were welcomed by the church, and the apostles and the elders; and they revealed what great things God had done with them' (15:4).

The next stage is a restatement of the difficulty: 'there arose some of the sect of the Pharisees, who had come to faith. They said, "It is necessary to circumcise them, and to order them to keep the Torah of Moses"' (15:5).

Stage three is discussion, among the 'apostles and the elders', in three parts: first, Peter argues (15:7-11) that both Jews and Gentiles, circumcised or not, have received the Holy Spirit; secondly, Paul and Barnabas (15:12), 'explained what great signs and portents God had worked among the Gentiles through them'. Thirdly, and rather surprisingly, James (15:13-21) comes down on the side of the more liberal side of the debate, with the result, finally, that the Jerusalem church composes a letter to send to Antioch with Paul and Barnabas, which limits Gentile obligations to the following (15:29):

> To refrain from eating food offered to idols, and from blood, and from meat that has been strangled, and from sexual immorality. If you keep yourselves free from these things, you will do well.

There is more to come, of course; but we should learn from the mood of attentive listening how to handle the painful issues of our own day.

The 'Rainbow Church'

One of the issues that can divide churches is the clash of cultures and languages; equally, however, it seems that what attracted people in vast numbers to the Jesus movement in that first century was the sense of 'Everyone belongs', or, as James Joyce put it, with regard to the Catholic Church, 'Here comes everybody.' You can see that in Antioch, where Luke tells us of the composition of the church officials. I mention these names here only because they are so telling, in the list of the 'prophets and teachers' there:

- Barnabas – an Aramaic name;

- Symeon – this name can be found in both Hebrew and Aramaic, but he has a nickname: Niger – the Latin for 'dark'; so this official has his feet in at least two cultures;

- Lucius – this is a Greek or Roman name, but we are also told that he is Cyrenean, so he is from Libya in North Africa;

- Menahem comes next, a good Hebrew name, and we are given a hint of his social status, in that he was 'brought up with Herod the tetrarch'; this is Herod Antipas, son of Herod the Great who, under the terms of his father's will, was tetrarch of Galilee (13:1).

This is a rich social and cultural mix.

Quarrels and tensions

In case you still need to be convinced that there were difficulties in the early Church, have a look at 15:36-40, where there is an apparently irreconcilable row between Barnabas and Paul over whether or not John Mark could be allowed to travel with them. He had abandoned them in Perga in Pamphylia, according to 13:13. Barnabas and Paul were never to work together again in Acts of the Apostles; although you may be relieved to see in 1 Corinthians 9:6 that the two of them are evidently on the same side; and possibly 2 Timothy 4:11 may imply that Paul and Mark were later reconciled.

We saw in the previous chapter that there had been tension between Paul and Apollos; this eloquent Alexandrian Jew is introduced to the reader of Acts at 18:24-28, where Priscilla and Aquila meet him in the synagogue in Ephesus, and give him a bit of remedial religious education. It must be said, however, that there is no sign of tension here.

There is a possible instance of tension, at Ephesus once more, when Paul meets up with some disciples (only 12!) of John the Baptist, who knew only of John's baptism, and had 'never even heard of the Holy Spirit', which in Acts suggests a woeful lack of catechesis; but there seems to be no tension here, and they apparently submit cheerfully enough to being 'baptised into the name of the Lord Jesus', and start speaking in tongues and prophesying (19:1-7).

Another story that I cannot resist because of the warning it offers to those who go in for preaching at great length (not so much a squabble, just a death by homily) is the story of the death and resuscitation of Eutychus, which the Christians of Troas seem to take quite calmly (20:7-12). There may be a hint of tension between Paul and his travelling companions in the next verse (20:13), when the companions go by boat to Assos while Paul goes overland, and then perhaps at Miletus, where Paul summons the elders of the church at Ephesus, rather than going to them, but Luke suggests that this was because Paul was in a hurry to get to Jerusalem for Pentecost (20:16-38).

In his speech to these elders, Paul uses what I call his 'commentator's future'[85] (20:30), when he tells the elders of Ephesus that 'men will arise from among

---

85. You will regularly hear in radio reports of matches in all sports a phrase that is grammatically future but is in fact describing the immediate past: 'X will take the ball and will go round Y and will pass to Z.' This is the 'commentator's future'.

you, speaking perverted things, to draw disciples behind them'. The reader is presumably to understand (or remember) that something of the sort has taken place in Ephesus. This is presumably an indication of some kind of tension in the early Church.

Paul ignores the warnings of the Spirit

Here is an odd indication of such tension, for at 21:4 we read of Paul being given warnings 'through the Spirit' against going to Jerusalem; and Agabus dramatically acts out Paul's future imprisonment in Jerusalem (21:10-14). Paul refuses to take any notice, and claims that 'I am ready not only to be imprisoned but also to die in Jerusalem, for the name of the Lord Jesus.' What should Paul have done?

The Spirit reaches Rome

Finally, at the end of Acts, and after many adventures, the gospel reaches Rome, where it has been headed all this time, and we read that the Roman Christians welcomed its messengers (28:15):

> The Christians having heard about us, came to meet us, as far as forum Appii and Tres Tavernae; when Paul saw them, he gave thanks to God, and took courage.

Conclusion

So Acts of the Apostles comes to its end, and we discover that even our divisions cannot stop the Spirit's journey.

Here are the final words of the journey (28:30, 31):

> Paul remained for two whole years at his own expense, and gave hospitality to all who journeyed into him, announcing the Kingdom of God, and teaching the things about the Lord Jesus Christ, with all confidence, without being prevented.

The last word of Acts is in Greek *akôlutôs*, which has to be translated into English by no fewer than three words ('without being prevented'). There is nothing at all, even our absurd divisions, that can stop the work of the Spirit. That is as true today as it was in the days of Paul's preaching and Luke's writing.

CHAPTER 5

The Johannine Literature

Introduction

We shall be looking in this chapter at a body of literature in the New Testament that carries clear marks of division, to see how its authors handled it; I say 'authors', because it is quite likely that the three Johannine epistles, even though they quite clearly come from the same stable, may well not have the same author as the fourth Gospel; but the question of authorship is irrelevant to our purpose at this point. The Book of Revelation is also in certain intriguing ways linked to these four documents, but we shall be looking at its attitude to divisions in a later chapter.

Before going to the texts, let me remind you of the observation of the aforementioned eminent lawyer who speaks of the Catholic Church's over-emphasis on what he calls 'pelvic sins', such as, for example, the unconventional domestic arrangements of those who are otherwise exemplary loving Catholics. He asks why is it only what goes on in the bedroom that has people clamouring for excommunication to be imposed?

This puzzle is an important one, because sometimes it seems that Christians can go in for a certain self-righteousness, feeling better because they can find other people to condemn; but they seem quite selective in the issues that they choose for this exclusionary policy. It may be good to bear this in mind as we read the Johannine Epistles and Gospel; for there are, as we shall see, plenty of hints of division here, but not on the kind of grounds that are familiar to us. There is much more on the identity of Jesus, and almost nothing on the 'pelvic area'.

2 John

We start by reading the two tiny fragments, perhaps the nearest that the New Testament gets to genuine letters, known as 2 and 3 John. Certainly there are hints of division here. Look at 2 John 4-6:

> I rejoiced very much because I found *some* of your children walking in truth, just as we received a command from the Father. And now I am asking you, Lady,[86] not as though I were writing you a new commandment;

---

86. In the first verse of the letter, the author addresses the recipient as 'Chosen Lady', which is often understood to be the particular church to whom he is writing, rather than a woman friend of the author.

no – it is the one that we had from the beginning, 'that we should love one another'. And this is what love is: that we should walk in accordance with his commandments, as you heard from the beginning, that you should walk in it.

The point here is that '*some* of your children' are 'walking in truth', which presumably carries the implication that others are not, and may carry a reminder that getting the commandments right has to do as much with behaviour as with belief. On this point you might think of John 3:21:

> The one who does Truth comes to the light, that his works may be revealed as being done in God.

This perhaps asserts the priority of orthopraxy over orthodoxy;[87] but the author of 2 John is also well aware of the need to get certain beliefs right, especially about Jesus, and that he has 'come in the flesh'. So in verse 7 we read that

> many imposters have come out into the world, those who do not admit that Jesus Messiah comes in the flesh. This is the person who is the imposter and Antichrist.

The fault-line here is the question of whether Jesus was really human, something on which Christians saw the need to insist from the very beginning. The opposite view, that Jesus only *seemed* to be human, is called Docetism (from a Greek word that means to 'seem'); it is the first Christian heresy, and is still alive and well today.

Then there is another category of people who divide the Church, namely 'everyone who is too go-ahead and fails to remain in the teaching'.[88] This is a familiar accusation in Christian circles; sometimes it is aptly levelled, sometimes it is not, but new thinking often causes divisions (which does not make it bad, of course). The sanction for this behaviour is fairly serious (10, 11):

> If someone comes to you and does not support this teaching, do not welcome that person into your home, and do not even give them greetings. For anyone who greets them shows solidarity with their evil deeds.[89]

This kind of excommunication has been all too common in the history of Christianity, and can still be found today. It does not sit well with the universal

---

87. Orthopraxy means getting our behaviour right, while orthodoxy means getting our thinking right.
88. Verse 9; you could translate the first word as 'going too far', possibly meaning those who are excessively 'progressive', or, in another form of discourse, too 'Modernist'.
89. Orthopraxy over orthodoxy once more, you see.

welcome of the early Church to all classes of society; but it may serve to remind us of the importance of understanding Jesus correctly.

3 John

This letter is addressed to 'beloved Gaius'. The latter is a very common Roman name and we would be wasting our time if we tried to identify this person with anyone else in the New Testament. We should notice, though, the characteristic Johannine expression of 'love', reinforced at the end of the verse: 'whom I love in truth'. Then the mood is reinforced when Gaius is once more addressed as 'beloved' at the beginning of verses 2, 5 and 11; and what has given rise to this 'love' is the report that 'I rejoice very much when fellow Christians come and give evidence of your Truth, that you are walking in Truth'. The author indicates that his greatest joy is 'that I hear my children are walking in Truth' (v.3). Doctrine and behaviour, orthodoxy and orthopraxy, run very close together here.

Later in the letter we see why this might be: it looks as though the Elder has written a letter (perhaps the document that we know as 1 John), and mentions someone called Diotrephes, about whom we know nothing, except that he is 'talking nonsense with wicked words' (v.10), and that 'he loves to be Number One', and in consequence 'does not accept us' (v.9). We can no longer reconstruct the problem, but there was clearly division in that community, for Diotrephes 'does not accept the brothers and sisters, and he hampers those who do want [presumably 'to receive them'] – and he throws them out of the Assembly'[90] (v.10). We are eavesdropping here on a painful moment in the history of the Church, even though we have only the remotest insight into the issue that was causing divisions. Diotrephes may have been the owner of the house where the church met, but we cannot say for certain. Unmistakably, though, this letter reinforces our general argument that there is nothing new about divisions in the Church. Our task is to handle them correctly. And lovingly.

1 John

This longest of the three 'epistles' is not really a letter at all, but some sort of theological treatise, urging the recipients to love and to get Jesus right. This note is sounded very early on in 1 John (1:3, 4):

> What we have seen and heard, we are announcing also to you, so that you also may have solidarity [*koinonia*, a word we have frequently heard before] with us. And our solidarity is with the Father and with his Son Jesus Messiah. And we are writing this to you that our joy may be fulfilled.

---

90. Or 'church'.

It is of immense importance to the author that 'solidarity' should be maintained in that church; and it has to do with the intimate link between Jesus and the Father that is so central to the theology of the Johannine community. The danger that the author envisages is that of 'walking in darkness', which is defined, as in 3 John, as when 'we lie and do not do the Truth' (1:6). It is hard to be sure what was the doctrinal position of the opponents, though when the author says that 'saying we are without sin' is 'self-deception', that may be what they are claiming (1:8-10). Above all, though, the way to cope with division is to 'remain in him', as we read at 2:4-6:

> The person who says 'I know him' and does not keep his commandments, is a liar; Truth is not in that person. But whoever keeps his word, the love of God is truly made perfect in that person. That is how we know we are in him. The one who claims to remain in him ought to walk/behave just as he walked/behaved.

Once again there is a link between orthopraxy and 'remaining in him', and presumably that is what the opponents failed to do. Another way of describing what they have got wrong is 'hating the fellow Christian' (v.11), which is made equivalent to 'remaining in darkness' or 'making them trip up'. Other metaphors for 'division' in chapter 2 include 'loving the world' (v.15), and not 'doing the will of God' (v.17); and our author dismisses the opponents as 'Antichrists' and treats them as evidence that 'it is the last hour', and their behaviour as evidence that 'they were not from us' (vv.18, 19). (One way of dealing with divisions, evident here, is to put a 'spin' on what others have done.) The author also introduces a label, 'the Liar', and defines it: 'the one who denies that Jesus is the Messiah . . . denying the Father and the Son' (v.22). Once again, we see that 'keeping eyes on God and on Jesus' is of major importance: 'everyone who denies the Son does not have the Father either; the one who acknowledges the Son has the Father also' (v.23). Clearly the author is convinced that the Church is in danger because of 'those who are leading you astray' (2:26), which suggests that there are several of these characters. He divides the world into two classes of being: those who do 'sin' or 'lawlessness' and those who do 'righteousness' or 'love of the brethren'. These two classes are described at 3:4-10:

> Everyone who does sin also does lawlessness. And Sin = Lawlessness. And you know that he was revealed in order that he might take away sins. And Sin is not in him. Everyone who remains in him does not sin; everyone who sins has not seen him or known him. Children, let no one lead you astray. The one who does righteousness is righteous, as that one is righteous.

The one who does Sin is from the Adversary, because the Adversary sins from the beginning.[91] The Son of God was revealed for this purpose, to undo the Adversary's works. Everyone who is born of God does not do Sin, because God's seed remains in that person, and that person cannot sin, because born from God. This is how God's children, and the children of the Adversary, are revealed: everyone who does not do righteousness is not from God; and [likewise] anyone who does not love their fellow Christian.

How do you know which side you are on? The author offers a clear test (4:2, 3):

This is how you know the Spirit of God: every spirit that acknowledges Jesus Messiah as having come in the flesh, is of God.

And every spirit that does not confess Jesus is not from God; and this is the spirit of the Antichrist (you have heard that he was coming; well, now he is already in the world).

Notice once again the insistence on the fleshly reality of Jesus' coming, and the importance of 'getting Jesus right'. Then the author offers another test: do they 'listen to us'? (4:6).

We are from God; the one who knows God listens to us; the one who is not from God does not listen to us.

That is how we know the Spirit of Truth and the spirit of deceit.

Above all, it is essential, according to 1 John, to 'get Jesus right': 'anyone who admits that Jesus is the Son of God, God remains in that person, and that person in God' (4:15); but it is also necessary to have the right attitude to fellow Christians: 'anyone who says "I love God", and who hates the brother or sister is a liar. For anyone who does not love the brother or sister, whom they have seen, cannot possibly love the God whom they have not seen' (4:20).

Finally, there is a question about what you do when fellow Christians sin (and increasingly we get the feeling that there was serious trouble in that early community) (5:16):

If someone sees the brother or sister sinning, a sin that is not 'towards death', they are to ask, and [God] will give them life, for those who do not sin 'towards death'. There is such a thing as a sin 'towards death'; I am not saying that they should ask about that one.

---

91. A clear reference to the 'beginning' of everything at John 1:1.

As so often in the New Testament, we find ourselves here listening to 'one side of the telephone conversation'; we have to admit that we do not know what is meant by the 'sin towards death'. In Catholic discourse, that was read as 'mortal sin'; but we do not know what the author and his original audience understood by it. The text gives the impression that both sides will have understood what is meant. For our purpose, what matters is the clear impression of the divisions that exist in the church that this document is addressing.

The Gospel of John

There are plenty of signs of division in the fourth Gospel; a good many of them have to do with the very high claims that Jesus makes in the course of it; and we should notice that it is always the religious people who get Jesus wrong. There may be a warning to us here, about the dangers of 'knowing that we are right'.

The word *schisma*, which we found three times in 1 Corinthians, makes its reappearance here, in the following places:

So there arose a *schisma* in the crowd because of him, [7:43, 44, immediately after they have argued about whether he was a prophet, or the Messiah, with the opposition certain that the Messiah has to come from Bethlehem, not Galilee] and some of them wanted to arrest him, but no one laid hands on him.

So some of the Pharisees started saying, 'This man is not from God, because he does not keep Sabbath.' But others were saying, 'How can a person who is a sinner do signs like this?' and there was a *schisma* among them [9:16, a passage that we shall look at later, in its broader context].

So there arose a *schisma* again among the Judeans, because of these words [10:19, where Jesus has just been laying claim to a very intimate relationship with the one whom he calls 'Father'].

It is worth noticing that all three of these uses of *schisma* are connected with the all-important question of who Jesus is, and the divisive nature of the claims made about him. It is not at all improbable that these controversies took place in Jesus' lifetime; but equally most scholars take the view that not all followers of Jesus, and perhaps especially within the Johannine community, were agreed on precisely what status to give him.

That may be what the marvellous Prologue to this fourth Gospel is getting at, when we read (1:10-11), of the Logos, that

he was in the world, and the world came to be through him,
and the world did not know him.
He came to his own, and his own did not accept him.

The 'world' in John's Gospel is somewhat ambiguous, but very often it represents the forces opposed to God's project; and here, right at the beginning of the Gospel, we are warned that the Logos (whom we know to be Jesus, though it nowhere actually says so) is going to be unacceptable to those ('his own') who might have been expected to welcome him. That is the context of all three of the uses of *schisma* that we quoted above.

We might also notice that the urgent questions of chapter 1 of John's Gospel (which can be seen as a kind of 'trying-on of hats', to get a feel of what titles fit Jesus) are very different ones from those to which the eminent lawyer cited at the beginning of this chapter was referring as 'pelvic'. So the questions on which John the Baptist is implicitly or explicitly interrogated at 1:19-25: 'Messiah?' 'Elijah?' 'The Prophet?' are Christological questions, rather than issues of sexual morality, but they have immense capacity to divide, as we shall see throughout the Gospel.

So the question of Jesus' identity is darkly shadowed, right from the start of the Gospel. Nathanael very sharply indicates that 'from Nazareth nothing good can come' (1:46),[92] and we are aware that this is a divisive question. We are therefore not altogether surprised when we hear at 2:18 that 'the Judeans said to him, "What sign do you show us, that you are doing these things?"' and discover that Jesus' death and resurrection are already on the agenda: 'Jesus was speaking of the Temple that was his body. So when he was raised from the dead, his disciples remembered that he was saying this, and they believed the scripture and the word that Jesus had said.'

One of the metaphors for the division over the identity of Jesus is that of light and darkness, which is first played out in the Prologue ['and the light shines in the darkness, and the darkness did not master it', 1:5, cf. verse 7]. So we go deeper into the mystery when at 3:19 we hear 'the light came into the world and people loved the darkness more than the light. For their works were evil.' And we shall do well to recall here the context, which is the visit that the semi-comprehending Nicodemus paid to Jesus, significantly 'by *night*' (3:2), in which the reader is easily able to understand the riddle which baffled Jesus' visitor: 'How can a person be born when they are old?'.

So division, on the controversial question of Jesus' identity, is evident from the very beginning of the fourth Gospel, and the way of overcoming

---

92. Compare 7:42, of course, and the assumption that the Messiah/Christ has to come from Bethlehem.

division is also there, as John the Baptist resolves a potential tension between his own disciples and Jesus, by saying (3:30), 'He must increase and I must decrease'. Eyes, you see, once more on Jesus, as the way of solving the problem of divisions.

The divisions in this Gospel are principally connected with the difficult question of Jesus' identity and his relationship to the one whom he calls 'Father'. See, for example, 5:18, after Jesus has, on the Sabbath, healed the paralysed person whom I call 'Old Grumpy': 'for this reason, the Judeans sought all the more to kill him; because not only did he undo the Sabbath; he also called God "his own Father" – making himself equal to God'. There is the real fault-line for John's Gospel (and perhaps also for us, if we really understood Jesus' claims). So in the speech that follows (5:19-47). Jesus makes clear the importance of listening to God and listening also to himself.

You get the same tension towards the end of chapter 6, where Jesus uses strong language to identify himself as 'Bread of Life':

So the Judeans muttered about him, because he had said 'I am the Bread of Life that is coming down from heaven' (6:41).

So the Judeans were fighting with each other, saying, 'How can this fellow give us his "flesh" to eat?' (6:52).

The inevitable result is that his hearers squabble about him, and there is something of this sort in our world today, of course. So it is not surprising that Jesus' claims are dismissed as a 'hard word' (6:60), and that when his support starts to ebb away, Jesus argues that 'one of you [the Twelve] is a devil', and we need to read and reflect upon Simon Peter's response to Jesus' sad question (6:66-9):

After this, many of his disciples went backwards and were no longer walking after him. So Jesus said to the Twelve: 'You don't also want to go away, do you?' Simon Peter answered him, 'Lord, to whom are we to go? You have the words of eternal life. And we have come to faith, and to know, that you are the Holy One of God.'

There is the way to end our divisions, once more: eyes on Jesus, eyes on God. Jesus always remains, however, a source of division in this Gospel (7:12):

There was great muttering about him among the crowds; some were saying 'He's good', while others were saying, 'No – he's leading the crowds astray.' But no one spoke openly about him, because of fear of the Judeans.

So there are always two views about him. Nor does Jesus make it easy for them, using very strong language such as this (8:44-7):

> You people are from your father, the Adversary, and you want to perform the desires of your father. He was a murderer from Day One, and did not take his stand in the Truth, because Truth is not in him. When he speaks falsehood, he speaks from what is his own, because he is false, and so is his father. But because I speak Truth, you people don't believe me. Who among you convicts me of sin? If I am talking Truth, why is it that you people don't believe me? The one who is from God hears God's words. That is why you people are not listening, because you are not from God.

The evangelist draws an unforgettable picture in chapter 9 of the blindness that afflicts people when they are faced with Jesus, and it may be helpful to read the whole of that remarkable, and remarkably crafted, chapter, to see the different kinds of blindness leading to division with which Jesus is faced.

The man born blind: a host of divisions

> And passing by, he saw a man who had been blind from birth. And they asked him, his disciples, saying, 'Rabbi, who sinned: was it this man or his parents, that he should be born blind?'

This is a dramatic story of divisions; and it starts with this idiot question (neither the first nor the last on their lips), which marks out the division between Jesus and his disciples. They do not reappear in the story.

> Jesus answered, 'It was not this one that sinned, nor his parents: it was in order that the works of God might be revealed in him. We must work the works of the One who sent me, while it is day. Night is coming when no one is able to work. When I am in the world, I am the light of the world.'

Jesus' response indicates why there are divisions about him; all the divisions have in the end to do with his identity, and his claim that there is One who sent him; once you deny that, divisions are inevitable.

> Saying this, he spat on the ground, and made mud out of the spittle; and he anointed his mud on the eyes. And he said to him, 'Off you go, wash in the pool of Siloam (which is translated 'Sent'). So he went off and washed, and came [back] seeing.

The striking thing here is how undramatic the miracle is: no magic wand or formula, and Jesus is not even present when it takes place – but notice the word

'Sent', which the evangelist links with the name of the pool. This brings together what Jesus has done to the man, and what the Father has done to Jesus.

> So the neighbours, and those who used to see him before (because he was a beggar) started saying, 'Isn't this the one who used to sit and beg?' Other people said, 'It's him', while others said, 'No – but it is someone like him.' But he was saying, 'I am.'

Now we see how the divisions start: could a miracle possibly have taken place? So there are disagreements about whether this person really has been cured. Notice what he says in response: 'I am', which on Jesus' lips is throughout the Gospel a very high claim indeed.[93] The formerly blind man is coming close to the only source of unity that matters.

> So they started saying to him, 'How were your eyes opened?' He answered, 'The man called Jesus made mud, and anointed my eyes and told me, "Go to Siloam and wash." So I went, and when I had washed, I recovered my sight.' And they said to him, 'Where is he?' He says, 'I don't know.'

The divisions continue, between the one who asserts that he has indeed been healed (but is forced at this stage to admit that 'I don't know'), and those who are committed to denying the implications of any such healing. He is simply reporting the facts.

> So they take him to the Pharisees (the chap who had been blind). Now it was Sabbath on the day when Jesus had made mud, and opened his eyes. So again the Pharisees also started asking him how he had recovered his sight. And he told them, 'He made mud on my eyes, and I washed and I see.' And so some of the Pharisees started saying, 'This man is not from God, because he does not keep Sabbath.' But others of them were saying, 'How can a person who is a sinner do such great signs?' And there was a *division* among them. So again they say to the blind man, 'What do you say about him, because he opened your eyes?' He said, 'He's a prophet.'

In the synoptic Gospels, when you hear the word 'Sabbath' and 'Pharisee' in the same sentence, you know that there is going to be trouble. The same theme operates here; but there is also the brute fact that a man who was blind is no longer so. Jesus' opponents start with their conclusion: 'This man is not from God', and interpret the fact in that light; others start with the fact and ask how

---

93. See 8:58 and 18:5, though English translations often conceal it under the guise of 'That's me.' And contrast Simon Peter's cowardly use of 'I am not' at 18:25.

Jesus can possibly be a sinner; then, once more, we meet our word *schisma*, as they pose the question to the blind man. He demonstrates that he is becoming less and less blind, by answering, 'He is a prophet', echoing the Samaritan woman (4:19), though he is shortly going to surpass her in his journey into sight.

> So the Judeans refused to believe about him, that he had been blind and had recovered his sight, until they summoned the parents (of the one who had recovered his sight), and asked them, saying, 'Is this your son, whom you say that he was born blind? How come he is seeing now?' So his parents replied and said, 'We know that this chap is our son, and that he was born blind – but how he sees now, we don't know. Ask him; he's old enough. He will speak for himself.' (The parents said this because they were afraid of the Judeans. For the Judeans had already come to an understanding that if anyone should acknowledge him as Messiah, they would be out of the synagogue. That was the reason why his parents had said, 'He's old enough – ask him.')

Now the divisions are made clear, and all Jesus' opponents can do is try to deny the fact, and so the man's parents are summoned. They reveal blindness of a different sort, by refusing to answer; the evangelist makes the point that it is really a question of Jesus' identity that is at issue here, with the reference to acknowledging him as 'Messiah', a grade above the identification of him as a prophet.

> So they summoned the man a second time (the one who had been blind), and they said to him, 'Give glory to God. We know that this man is a sinner.' So he said to them: 'I don't know whether he is a sinner. One thing that I do know: I was blind, and now I am seeing.' So they said to him, 'What did he do to you? How did he open your eyes?' He answered them, 'I told you already, and you didn't listen. Why do you want to hear it again? You don't want to become disciples of him, do you?' And they abused him and said, '*You're* a disciple of *him*; but we are disciples of *Moses*. *We*[94] know that to Moses God spoke; but this one – we don't know where[95] he is from.' The man answered and said, 'Now there's a remarkable thing: you people don't know where he is from – and he opened my eyes! We know that God does not listen to sinners; but if someone is God-fearing, and does God's will, then God listens to that person. Since the beginning of time it is unheard of that anyone opened the eyes of someone born blind. If this chap were not from God, he could not have done a thing.'

94. The series of words in italics is a slightly clumsy way of indicating the evangelist's emphatic use of personal pronouns.
95. 'where from', here and in the next sentence, represents a single interrogative word in Greek; you might translate it 'whence', to get the effect. It is a really important question in John's Gospel, though we do not often notice it.

The divisions continue, and Jesus' opponents couch their division in pseudo-religious language: 'give glory to God', and proclaim Jesus' identity ('a sinner'); the blind man insists on the fact: I was blind and now I see. They cannot accept this, and demand to hear the story again, which leads to the question of discipleship (the choice for the reader: Jesus or Moses?). Again the blind man insists on the fact ('he opened my eyes') and its implication for the divisive question of Jesus' identity. He is now unashamedly articulating the theology of John's Gospel: Jesus must be from God.

> They responded to him, 'Were you utterly born in sin, and are *you* teaching *us*?' And they expelled him. Outside.

The only possible response of the opponents is denial and excommunication. This is precisely how *not* to exercise religious authority.

> Jesus heard that they had expelled him outside; and when he had found him, he said, 'Do you believe in the Son of Man?' He answered and said, 'And who is it, Lord, that I may believe in him?' Jesus said to him, 'Not only have you seen him, but the one talking to you is him.' He said, 'I believe, Lord'. And he worshipped him.

Jesus heals the division by taking the excommunicated and no-longer-blind person a stage further into the revelation, by introducing a further title, after 'prophet' and 'man sent from God' – namely, 'Son of Man', the title that formed the climax of the Christological revelation ('trying-on of hats') in chapter 1 (v.51), where it is the very last word.

> And Jesus said, 'It was for judgement that I came into this world, that those who do not see might see and those who see might become blind.'

This more or less brings the story to an end, with the final verdict on the divisions over Jesus' identity.

> Some of the Pharisees who were with him heard this, and said, '*We're* not blind, are we?'

But the divisions persist, with the denial of blindness.

> Jesus said to them, 'If you were blind, you would have no sin. But as it is, you say, "We see" – your sin remains.'

A word of warning, this, to religious people who have the dangerous certainty that they know it all. Getting Jesus right can be a very divisive thing.

The shepherd picture

One of the great images for unity in the fourth Gospel is that of the flock gathered around the shepherd. There are different ways of being a shepherd. The theme is played in chapter 10. Significantly, perhaps, the first time it appears it is in terms of the opposite of the shepherd, the 'thief and brigand' (10:1):

> Amen, amen I am telling you, the one who does not come through the gate into the sheepfold but comes up from elsewhere is thief and brigand.

He is then immediately contrasted with 'the shepherd of the sheep', the one who comes 'through the gate' (10:2). Then we hear our familiar slogan of 'eyes on Christ' (10:3-5):

> His sheep hear his voice; and he calls his own sheep by name, and leads them out. When he takes out all his own [sheep] he marches before them, and his sheep follow him, because they know his voice. They will not follow a stranger. No – they will run away from him, because they do not recognise the voice of strangers.

The profound unity among the sheep echoes the unity between the Father and the Son ('eyes on Jesus, eyes on God'), and the high price to be paid for unity (10:14, 15):

> I am the Real Shepherd, and I know my [sheep] and mine know me, just as the Father knows me and I know the Father. And I lay down my life for the sheep.

It does not stop there, however, for, very importantly, the shepherd looks beyond the immediate flock (10:16):

> And I have other sheep, who are not of this fold, and I must lead them; and they will listen to my voice, and they shall become one flock, one shepherd.

Again and again, it is the Christological assertions of John's community that causes division, so when Jesus makes the very strong claim that 'the Father and I are one', he elicits a very strong reaction (10:31-3):

> So the Judeans picked up stones once more, in order to stone him. Jesus answered them, 'I showed you many good works from my Father. For which of these works are you stoning me?' The Judeans answered him, 'We are not stoning you for a "good work", but for blasphemy, and because you, who are a human being, are making yourself a "god".'

Nor is it solely Jesus' opponents who are divided about him. In chapter 11, the disciples think that he is crazy when he announces his intention, after some delay, of going to see the sick Lazarus (11:8):

> His disciples say to him, 'Rabbi, the Judeans were just now looking to stone you. And are you going there again?'

Then Thomas, who is something of a character in the fourth Gospel, but not in the synoptics, joins in the general disapproval (11:16):

> So Thomas, the one called 'Twin', said to his fellow disciples, 'Why don't we go too, so as to die with him?'

In the same chapter, both of Lazarus' sisters accuse Jesus of neglecting them:

> So Martha said to Jesus, 'Lord, if you had been here, my brother would not have died' (11:21).

> So when Mary came to where Jesus was, when she saw him, she fell at his feet, saying to him, 'Lord, if you had been here, my brother would not have died' (11:32).

In the first case, that led to a very profitable theological discussion, culminating in Jesus' affirmation to Martha that 'I am the Resurrection and the Life'. In the second case, it leads to Jesus 'snorting' (11:33, 38) and enduring the disbelief of the Judean crowds who were mourning with Martha and Mary, but eventually to a prayer to his Father, and then the raising of Lazarus.

The Last Supper discourse

Then there is the Last Supper, where once again there is tension between Jesus and his followers, for example, when 'the devil had already flung it into the heart of Judas son of Simon Iscariot that he should betray him' (13:2); and the tension is even more acute when Jesus offers his model of service (13:6-8):

> He rises from the supper, and takes off his clothes, and taking a linen cloth he put it on himself. Then he throws water into the washbasin and began to wash the feet of the disciples, and to wipe them with the linen cloth in which he was clad. And so he comes to Simon Peter. He says to him, 'Lord – are *you* washing *my* feet?' Jesus said to him, 'What I am doing you do not understand for the moment; but you will know later on.' Peter says to him, 'No way are you going to wash my feet. Ever.'

John's Last Supper discourse begins (13:1) and ends (17:24, 26) with love, and the idea runs throughout the five chapters. That does not, however, mean that there are no divisions. As we have seen, Judas is on his way to betray Jesus, and Peter has only a very limited understanding of the mystery; perhaps worse than that, Jesus announces (13:21) that 'one of you is going to betray me'; then he identifies Judas as the traitor (though the Beloved Disciple does not appear to pass on the information to anyone). What is significant, perhaps, is that Jesus does nothing to prevent the treachery taking place; indeed, when Judas goes out into the night (13:30), Jesus' entirely unexpected comment is, 'Now the Son of Man has been glorified, and God has been glorified in him.' Unusually, the fourth Gospel depicts the cross as a throne of glory, rather than as the bleak disaster that it is for Mark. It is therefore just possible that we should be fairly calm about our scandal of Christian disunity; God can work even through our disasters.

Not that we should be too ready to let ourselves off, however. For the theme of love is not just about God and Jesus; it concerns us too (13:34, 35):

> I am giving you a new commandment, that you should love each other, just as I loved you, that you too may love each other. That is how everyone will know that you are my disciples, if you have love for each other.

Above all, and this should be our way of coping with Christian disunity, it is our task to love Jesus, and hence the Father, as the Lord makes clear, first in response to Jude's 'idiot question', and second in pursuit of the image of the 'vine':

> 'If a person loves me, they will keep my word, and my Father will love that person, and we shall come to them and make a dwelling with them. The one who does not love me does not keep my words. And the word that you are hearing is not mine – it belongs to the One who sent me, the Father' (14:23, 24).

> 'This is my commandment, that you love each other as I loved you. No one has greater love than this, than that a person lays down their life for their friends. You are my friends if you do what I am commanding you. I am no longer calling you "slaves", because a slave does not know what his lord is doing. I have called you "friends", because I made known to you everything that I heard from my Father. It was not you that chose me. No – it was I who chose you. And I have placed you for you to go and bear fruit, and for your fruit to remain, in order that whatever you ask the Father in my name he may give you. This is what I am commanding you, to love each other' (15:12-17).

So the appropriate response of Christians to their scandalous brokenness is to put their lives on the line, out of love. And it is our task to leave our mark on the world ('bear fruit'). There is no pretence, however, that we are particularly good at remaining faithful: 'the hour is coming, and has arrived, for you each to be scattered to your own, and leave me alone. And [yet] I am not alone, because my Father is with me' (16:32).

Nevertheless, the evangelist wishes us to be aware of the dangers of disunity; Jesus prays, in the final chapter of the Last Supper discourse, the so-called 'High Priestly prayer' to the Father, 'that they may be one as we are one', and the great discourse ends with emphasis on unity, based on that between the Father and the Son (17:20-26):

> I am not asking about these alone, but also about those who come to faith in me through their word, that they may all be one, as you, Father, are in me and I am in you, that they too may be in us, that the world may believe that it was you who sent me. And the glory that you have given to me, I have given to them, that they may be one as we are one, I in them and you in me, so that they may be made perfect into one, that the world may know that it was you who sent me and loved them as you loved me. Father, what you have given me, I wish that where I am they may be also with me, that they may see my glory, which you have given me because you loved me before the foundation of the world. Righteous Father: the world also did not know you, but I knew you. And these know that it was you who sent me. And I made known your name to them, and I shall continue to make it known, that the love with which you loved me may be in them and I may be in them.

In all the Gospels the disciples make inadequate responses (so perhaps we should not be too hard on ourselves because of our disunity), as in the following example. The violent person is anonymous in the synoptics; only the fourth Gospel names him as Peter; but it is clearly an inappropriate response to the arrest of Jesus (18:10, 11):

> So Simon Peter, who had a sword [why, for heaven's sake??] drew it and struck the slave of the High Priest, and cut off his earlobe, the right-hand one. And the slave's name was Malchus. So Jesus said to Peter, 'Put your sword into its sheath: the cup that the Father has given me, am I not to drink it?'

One tiny episode, however, reminds us of the importance of unity among the successors of Jesus (19:25-7):

There stood by the cross of Jesus his mother and his mother's sister, Mary of Clopas and Mary the Magdalene. So Jesus, seeing his mother, and the disciple standing by, the one whom he loved, says to his mother, 'Woman – look: your son.' Then he says to the disciple, 'Look: your mother.' And from that hour the disciple took her to his own.

The point here is that if Jesus' group is to continue they have to be united, after the disaster of his death.[96] The mother of Jesus appears in John's Gospel only here, at the very end, and at the very beginning, at the wedding feast of Cana (2:1-11). In neither place is she named; but she brackets his entire mission, and here is seen as part of the dynasty that continued it. We should also notice the Beloved Disciple; this figure in some ways stands for the ideal reader of the Gospel, but here we read that 'he took her *to his own*', *in* contrast to what we have just heard about the disciples at large, who Jesus predicts will be 'scattered *to your own*' (16:32). And, of course, we remember the words of the Prologue to the Gospel: '[the Word] came *to his own*, and *his own* did not receive him' (1:11). Here the process is reversed, and the unity of mother and Beloved Disciple enables the message to continue.

Likewise, two relatively obscure disciples of Jesus engage in teamwork to give him an appropriate burial, modelling the kind of behaviour that should be detectable in us (19:38-42):

After this, Joseph, the one from Arimathea, who was a disciple of Jesus (but a hidden one, because of fear of the Judeans), asked Pilate if he might take the body of Jesus; and Pilate gave his permission. So he came and took his body. And Nicodemus came too, the one who had come to him by night, the first time, with a mixture of myrrh and aloes (about 100 litres!). So they took Jesus' body and wrapped it in linen cloths, with spices. And there was in the place where he had been crucified, a garden, and in the garden a new tomb, in which no one had ever been laid. And so there, because of the preparation day of the Judeans, because the tomb was nearby, they laid Jesus.

In the following chapter, it is not precisely a team, but three different agents, between whom there might be tension, who seem to have got it right by the end (20:1-10):

On the first day of the week, Mary the Magdalene comes early, while it was still dark, to the tomb; and she sees the stone rolled away from the

---

96. For it is a disaster, even if the fourth Gospel presents it as a triumph.

tomb. So she runs and comes to Simon Peter, and to the other disciple, whom Jesus loved, and says to them, 'They have taken the Lord out of the tomb, and we do not know where they have placed him.' So Peter and the other disciple came out, and they were going towards the tomb. The two of them were running together. And the other disciple ran more quickly than Peter. And he came to the tomb first. Then he stooped down and sees the cloths lying there. But he did not go in. So Simon Peter also comes, following him. And he went into the tomb, and sees the cloths lying, and the sweat-cloth, which was not lying with the cloths, but apart, rolled up in one place. So then the other disciple also went in, the one who had arrived first at the tomb. And he saw, and he believed. For they did not yet know the Scripture that he must rise from the dead. So the disciples went off home.

Mary was there first (as all the Gospels agree), and the Beloved Disciple, with his greater closeness to Jesus, came second, but graciously let Simon Peter, the future leader of the Church, precede him. The two males then go home, leaving Mary weeping outside the tomb, and encountering angels and ultimately Jesus himself (though she at first thought he was a passing gardener); then at the end it is once more Mary Magdalene who becomes the apostle to the disciples ('I have seen the Lord', 20:18), and therefore she is, if anything, more important than the two males.

The next point to observe is the Thomas episode. At 20:19-23 we are given an account of the appearance of Jesus to the fearful (v.19) and unbelieving (the clear implication of verse 20) disciples. Then it turns out that Thomas, who, as we have already seen, is something of a character in this Gospel, was for some reason absent from this appearance. They cannot resist gloating over him ('We've seen the Lord', v.25), at which he makes a most brutal demand, underlining the divisions and inadequacies of the disciples: 'Unless I see in his hands the mark of the nails, and throw my finger into the mark of the nails and throw my hand into his side, no way am I going to believe.' Inevitably, a second appearance, a week later, challenges him to do precisely that, and his response (once more 'eyes on Jesus') puts all tensions and divisions away, with the astonishing verdict, the high point of the Christology of the fourth Gospel: 'My Lord and my God' (20:28).

There remains just one chapter of this Gospel, the last, sometimes thought to come from a different author, although the style of the Greek suggests otherwise. From our point of view, the interest lies in the reaction between the two principal characters, Peter and the Beloved Disciple, and their Lord, where all tensions are finally swept away. Led by Peter (21:3) some, though not all, of the Twelve, are out fishing, which suggests perhaps a gloomy return to their original trade; then they encounter Jesus (without recognising him, however) and have a miraculous catch of fish. The Beloved Disciple works out what is going on, and tells Peter, 'It is the Lord', which leads Simon into some idiotic behaviour, such as putting his clothes *on* (rather than taking them off) in order to plunge into the sea, even though it turns out that the boat is hardly any distance from the shore.

Then, however, comes a conversation which Simon Peter may have been dreading, since it is not all that long since he was denying that he was a disciple of Jesus (18:17, 25, 27), and the question, not a bad one under the circumstances, is posed (21:15-17):

> 'Simon, son of John, do you love me more than these?' He says to him, 'Yes, Lord, you know that I love you.' He says to him, 'Feed my lambs.'
>
> He says to him again, a second time, 'Simon, son of John, do you love me?' He says to him, 'Yes Lord. You know that I love you.' He says to him, 'Shepherd my sheep.'
>
> He says to him the third time, 'Simon, son of John, do you love me?' Peter was grieved that he had said to him for the third time, 'Do you love me?' and he says to him, 'Lord, you know everything, you know that I love you.' Jesus says to him, 'Feed my sheep.'

What is going on here? This interchange is followed by what the evangelist interprets (21:19) as a prediction of the kind of death that Peter would experience. Scholars have made a good deal of the fact that two different words for 'love' are used, and it has been suggested that what Jesus first asks is whether Peter is capable of really unselfish love, and that by the end all he is capable of is 'friendship', which is a lesser form of it. Sadly, I do not think that this is the case; it is true that the two words are used, but John frequently does that, when there is no difference in meaning; he just likes synonyms. For example, see the three instructions that Peter is given: 'feed my lambs', 'shepherd my sheep' and 'feed my sheep'. These are clearly identical in content, but for elegance expressed differently on each occasion. More germane to our purposes is the fact that Simon Peter is invited to express his love in terms of looking after those for whom the 'Real Shepherd' of chapter 10 originally came, and preserving their unity.

Conclusion

So at the end of this gallop through the Johannine literature, what can we say? Certainly the community knows of divisions, both in its history and in the lifetime of Jesus and his first group; so we are not to feel too alarmed by the divisions we see today. At the same time, however, they had to deal with them, and we have seen that they are to do this by keeping their eyes on God and on Jesus, and by a readiness even to die for one another. Those are good remedies for us today.

CHAPTER 6

Handling divisions in Mark's Gospel

In this chapter we shall be looking at how the first Gospel to be written handled the divisions that (as we have been arguing) have always been a part of the Church's history. There are, so far as I can see, three kinds of division in this pioneering Gospel. First there are the divisions between Jesus and the religious authorities of the Judaism from which Jesus emerged. Here we should notice that these authorities were not wrong in the points that they made against Jesus; they were accurate in pointing to 'what the Bible says'. The second kind of division is that between Jesus and his 'family'; and the third, perhaps most alarming for us, are the divisions among Jesus' disciples or between Jesus and his disciples. In each case, of course, we are invited to recognise ourselves, and the contributions that we have made to divisions in the Church.

Divisions between Jesus and religious authorities

We start with the divisions between Jesus and the religious authorities. A warning bell rings quite early, at 1:22, where we read that he was teaching 'with authority, not like the scribes'. This is the first time that these characters have been mentioned; and who are they? They possess the rare gift of being able to decipher marks on papyrus, and of being able to make such marks, the precious gift of literacy. That, in such a world, gave them immense power and authority, and since the main texts in such a world were what we call 'scripture', they were able to say, 'This is what God says,' and, 'These are God's rules.' In Mark's Gospel we shall find that for the most part they represent opposition to Jesus, who, it seems, sat lightly to the skills of reading and writing, and to questions about 'the rules'. The scribes then reappear at the end of Jesus' first 'busy day', when the paralysed man is let down through the roof by his friends, and in response to Jesus' unexpected remark, 'Child – your sins are forgiven,' they appear from nowhere and we are permitted to hear them asking (2:7), 'Why is this man talking like this? He is blaspheming! Who can forgive sins except One, [namely] God?' At this point we sense that death is on the way, for 'blasphemy' is a capital offence, and indeed Jesus will later on be convicted on that charge (14:61-4). So right from the beginning we feel the tension between Jesus and the religious authorities.

This continues a little bit later in chapter 2, when we meet the 'scribes of the Pharisees' (we know, even without having met these characters before, that they mean trouble), who express their displeasure at Jesus' 'terrible friends': 'with tax collectors and sinners he eats?' (2:16). This is then followed by a complaint, just the sort of thing that good religious people go in for (2:18): 'Why do the disciples of John and the Pharisees' disciples fast – but your disciples do not fast?' Later in the chapter the tension rises further, as Jesus' disciples are doing what is not lawful on the Sabbath (2:23), plucking ears of corn. And from now on, virtually every time we meet one of these religious figures, the divisions deepen, and start to lead unmistakably towards death. So the very next episode has Jesus in the synagogue on the Sabbath, and in the presence of a man with 'a dried up hand', and Mark tells us that 'they were watching him', which conveys a clear sense of hostility; this is confirmed when you hear the evangelist continue, 'to see if he was going to heal on the Sabbath, in order that they might make an accusation against him'. Religious people can behave in this way, all too often.

Jesus first sets the stage: 'He says to the man who has the dried up hand, "Rise up into the middle."' Then he asks a devastating question: 'Is it permitted, *on the Sabbath* (this phrase is positioned emphatically in the sentence, hence the italics), to do good or to do evil? To save life or to kill?' There is no response, or rather the response is an angry taciturnity: 'They were silent.' Why do I say angry? See what happens next: 'He looked around them with rage, grieving over the hardness of their hearts,' then Mark makes us focus once more on the man, who is still standing there, and whom Jesus tells: 'Stretch out your hand.' He does so and (of course) 'his hand was restored'. And the upshot? 'The Pharisees immediately went out with the Herodians, and made a plot against him, how to destroy him.' It ends, you see, in death, plotted by two unlikely yoke-fellows, since the Pharisees stood for freedom as a people for God, and the Herodians (presumably, we cannot be sure) for accommodating with Rome. Nevertheless, Jesus has done enough for both of them to want him dead.

There is another way of expressing opposition, and in that culture it is equally lethal, which we encounter when we discover that 'the scribes, the ones who had come down from Jerusalem, started saying, "He has Beelzeboul" and, "It's by the Ruler of demons that he throws out demons"' (3:22). In very many cultures the allegation of using evil spirits is very dangerous indeed. Jesus effortlessly rebuts the charge (3:23-7), but it remains a sinister presence, hanging in the air. Have you ever experienced something like this in your own discipleship?

In chapter 7, they are at it again, these religious people, taking offence at Jesus, by way of his disciples, because they are not sufficiently religious; in this case they are failing to do what good religious people do, by way of washing before meals, and 'maintaining the tradition of the elders' (7:3). So the question is put to Jesus: 'Why do your disciples not walk in accordance with the tradition of the elders, and instead eat food with profane hands?' Jesus accuses them of being 'hypocrites' (a Greek word meaning 'actors', and a common weapon to wield against religious people), and quotes his beloved Isaiah, accusing them of preferring their own traditions to God's will, in a devastating argument that should have all religious people feeling the challenge. This is not, you see, just a story about long ago; it is acted out every day between those who are certain about how religious people should behave, and those who hear God urging them to march to the beat of a different drum.

Something of this is going on the next time we see Jesus in dialogue (perhaps that is not quite the right word) with the religious authorities, in the shape of the Pharisees. For immediately after Jesus has fed the 4000 (8:1-10), Mark shows these very religious people demanding a sign from Jesus; as he tells the story, it seems that feeding the crowds so abundantly does not count. And Jesus simply refuses to play their game: 'He groaned in his spirit and says to them, "Why does this generation look for a sign? Amen I'm telling you, if a sign will be given to this generation . . . "'

The next time we see them (10:2-12), the Pharisees are raising a question that is still with us today: 'Is it permitted for a man to divorce his wife?' Jesus interrogates them about the Law, which elicits the response that in Deuteronomy Moses permits divorce 'on account of your hardness of hearts', and we can see the divisions becoming ever deeper, as Jesus quotes Scripture back at them: 'Male and female [God] created them. Therefore a man will leave his mother and father and stick to his wife. And the two shall become one flesh.' Jesus' astonished disciples ask him about this, and are told, 'Whoever divorces his wife and marries another woman, commits adultery upon her.' This is still a live issue in our day, of course; and Christianity stands for a value of immense importance when it insists that marriage is for life; but we might notice that the question as posed concerns men divorcing women. So it may not be precisely dealing with the issue that we suppose to be on the table here; rather the question may be one of how women are to be treated in a patriarchal society. At all events, we need to use Jesus as our model in dealing with divisive religious questions, not in anger and hatred but in love and with reason.

We can feel the divisions with the religious authorities growing as the Gospel goes on. Our next encounter is after Jesus' dramatic gesture in the Temple (11:15-19), when he 'began to expel the sellers and buyers', with the result that 'the Chief Priests and the scribes heard, and started to look for a way to destroy him', even though 'they were afraid of him'. From this point onwards the tension mounts slowly, and death is the only way out. So the authorities approach him 'in the Temple', a significant place to pick a battle, for it is their territory, not that of the pious Galilean peasant: 'They approached, the Chief Priests and the scribes and the elders, and they said to him "By what authority are you doing these things? Or who gave you this authority, that you should do them?"' The attentive reader knows that Jesus is acting by God's authority, and has been aware of this from the very beginning of the Gospel. So we applaud as Jesus throws the question back at them, asking, 'John's baptism – was it from heaven, or from human beings?' They are for the moment silenced and refuse to reply; Jesus triumphantly concludes: 'And neither am I saying to you by what authority I am doing these things' (11:27-33).

Sadly, though, this does not defeat them, and Jesus does not hold back as he lays into them with the parable of the vineyard and the tenants (12:1-12), which makes it clear that they are opposing God and bent on destroying God's son. At the end of this story, we read that 'they abandoned him, and went away', but we know that they have not conceded; so we are not surprised when this encounter is followed immediately by the lethal question (12:13-17) posed by the 'Pharisees and Herodians' once more, about whether it is permissible to pay tax to Caesar. Jesus effortlessly answers them, but wins no friends in responding as he does: 'The things that belong to Caesar, give to Caesar, and the things that belong to God – give to God!'

The Pharisees and Herodians are immediately followed by Sadducees, the priestly aristocracy who ran the Temple. Their question is one about resurrection (in which they do not believe); once again, Jesus effortlessly answers them, brilliantly citing Exodus 3:2, which works well because the Sadducees, unlike the Pharisees, only accept the first five books of the Torah. However, death is now clearly on the agenda, and talk of resurrection may seem like an empty consolation. We are therefore not at all surprised by the next encounter with the religious authorities, with the High Priest and the Sanhedrin, which Mark recounts at 14:55-65. The growing tension with the religious authorities comes to its climax at this point; we hear that murder is unequivocally on the agenda ('they were looking for evidence against Jesus, in order to put him to death – and they couldn't find any', 14:55, and compare 14:1 for the lethal intent). When it seems that no evidence is going to be forthcoming, the High Priest takes a hand: 'he rose up into the middle, and interrogated Jesus'. The question he puts is one that any reader of Mark could answer: 'Are you the Messiah, the Son of the Blessed One?'

Then he gets what he is looking for, as Jesus draws himself up to his full height and declares: 'I AM. And [here quoting Daniel 7:13] you are going to see the Son of Man sitting on the right hand of Power, and coming with the clouds of heaven.' At that point the High Priest has got what he was looking for, and declares a verdict: 'blasphemy'; so the court obediently passes sentence (or is it another verdict?) that he is 'guilty of death', and fall to 'hooding' Jesus and slapping him, and telling him to 'prophesy', as a preliminary to death (by way of a trial before Pilate).

They appear one last time, these religious authorities, when Jesus is finally crucified (15:31, 32):

> The High Priests mocked him antiphonally with the scribes, and started saying, 'He saved others – he can't save himself! Let the Messiah, the "King of Israel" come down, now, from the cross, that we may see and believe.'

The divisions have reached their peak, and Jesus is finally rejected by the very religious authorities whom he might have expected to be open to his message. It is a desperately sad story, and the divisions are at this point immensely, bleakly, painful.

It is not quite as simple, however, as simply dismissing all religious authorities as hostile to Jesus' (and God's) project, for there are two very deceptive moments. The first takes place as Jesus gets off a boat on the Sea of Galilee, at 5:22; as he disembarks, there appears 'one of the synagogue rulers'. Now we have learned in this Gospel to expect trouble at the mention of 'synagogue', so we are expecting some kind of trap. But the pattern is broken by the simple fact that we are given his name, Jairus, which means something like '[God] will give light'; and we are won over to his side by the fact that 'he falls at [Jesus'] feet, and begged him greatly, saying, "My daughter is at her last extremity, [I'm asking] that you should come and lay hands on her, that she may be saved and live."' We know as soon as we hear this petition that all is going to be well; and so it turns out, as Jesus goes to his house and, although the daughter has now died, she is effortlessly restored to life, and given to her parents, with an instruction to feed her (5:35-42). So it is not the case that every single instance of a religious ruler turns out to be opposed to Jesus' project.

We see this quite strikingly in another story, in chapter 12, immediately after the raising of the tension in the stories that we were looking at a few moments ago. The last story has a 'scribe' approaching and joining in the argument. We assume that once more this will be an attempt to get Jesus, especially when we hear him asking, 'Which commandment is Number One of all?' There were 613 commandments, and it was a minefield trying to prioritise them; but as the story develops (12:28-34) we discover that there is a wholly unexpected meeting of minds, as the scribe praises Jesus for quoting the Shema in his answer, and giving not one but two commandments. Jesus then responds (and it is quite a shock to us): 'You are not far from the Kingdom of Heaven.' So, once again, we are not permitted to dismiss all religious people as endeavouring to kill Jesus.

Divisions between Jesus and his 'family'

Then comes a second set of divisions in Mark's Gospel, between Jesus and his 'family'. Once again we are invited to ask if we recognise ourselves in these stories. These divisions appear just three times.

The first time is in chapter 3, when (as we saw above) the tension is beginning to mount. He comes in verse 20 'to a house', followed, doubtless to the householder's irritation, by 'the crowd', so that 'they were unable even to eat a loaf of bread'. Then we get the reaction of his intimates: 'When they heard, his people came out to arrest him – for they said, "He has lost his senses."' Here the charge of insanity springs apparently from the failure to eat (if it was Jesus and his disciples), because in that culture it is your responsibility to make sure that your family eats, and you are shamed if they do not. And who is doing the arresting? The phrase that I have translated as 'his people' literally means 'those from him', and that could be family or friends. The point as far as we are concerned is that Jesus is and always has been a divisive figure.

The second example of this division is much more clearly his family. Later in the chapter, after he has been insultingly accused by the scribes of 'having Beelzeboul', his 'mother and his brothers come, and standing outside they sent to him, calling him' (3:31). This is clearly a scene of some tension, and suggests an anxiety about what he is up to. Then Mark's camera focuses on the crowd, which 'sat around him' (as opposed to 'standing outside'), and pass on the message: 'Look! Your mother and your brothers and sisters are outside, looking for you.'

Jesus' response is not encouraging: 'Who are my mother and my brothers?' Then he redefines family: 'Looking around at those sitting about him in a circle, he says, "Look at my mother and my brothers. For whoever does God's will, that person is my brother and sister and mother."' There are divisions here, even if we cannot say precisely what is at issue between him and his family.

The third instance of division is to be found at 6:1-6, where Jesus returns from somewhere by the Sea of Galilee to his homeland, which is presumably Nazareth, although the evangelist does not say so. What he does is have Jesus reflect ruefully on the situation: 'a prophet is not without honour except in his home territory, and among his kinsfolk and in his own household', a saying that is echoed (unusually) in John's Gospel (John 4:44). Here it is not the family that reject him, though they may be contrasted unfavourably with him: 'Is not this the carpenter, the son of Mary and the brother of Jacob and Joses and of Judas and of Simon? And are not his sisters here with us?' The division is really with his local compatriots, rather than the family; but, once again, the point seems to be that Jesus is a divisive figure.

Divisions between Jesus and his disciples

The final set of divisions that run through this Gospel is, sadly, between Jesus and his disciples. It might be worth noticing that these divisions are more common in the second half of the Gospel, after 8:27, than in the first half; it is possible that Mark was writing to encourage a generation of disciples who had proved unfaithful under the pressure of persecution, to show them that Jesus' first disciples were no better. As always, we must be prepared to recognise ourselves in these unworthy models of discipleship.

This process starts already in the first half of the Gospel. The first time we see it is at 1:35-8. Jesus goes off in the early morning to pray, and then we learn that 'Simon and those with him hunted him down', which is clearly not what is supposed to happen, since the instructions to Simon, back in 1:17, were not, 'Hunt me down whenever you feel like it', but 'Come here, after me and I am going to make you into fishers of human beings.' Jesus does not here waste time rebuking them, but, in response to their reproach ('They're all looking for you'), he simply says, 'Let's go elsewhere, to the cities round about, that I may give the message there. For this is why I came.' The misunderstanding is dealt with by means of another invitation.

The next time we see signs of division between Jesus and his followers is after the first of his parables, at the beginning of chapter 4, when 'those around him with the Twelve asked about the parables' (in other words, 'What *are* you talking about?', 4:10). There is just a hint of rebuke here, which is repeated, more urgently this time, at the end of that chapter (4:35-41), when they are in a boat, and Jesus is fast asleep. So they arouse him (Mark uses a resurrection word here) and ask, angrily or in terror, and certainly aggressively, 'Teacher, don't you *care* that we are being destroyed?' (4:38). Jesus simply gives orders to the sea and the wind, with immediate effect, and accuses the disciples of cowardice and lack of faith; and the aggressive disciples are left in deep awe ('they feared a great fear'): 'So who is this, that even the wind and the sea obey him?' Their aggression is deflated.

In the next chapter, in the story of the woman with the haemorrhage, they are once again guilty of an inappropriate response. At 5:27 the woman touches Jesus' garment, and is instantly healed; in the next verse, Jesus feels the power going out of him, and turns round in the crowd, asking, 'Who touched my clothing?' The disciples more or less jeer at him: 'You see the crowd pressing upon you, and you're saying, "Who touched me?".' They are out of sympathy with Jesus, who simply ignores them, and continues to look for 'the woman who had done this'.

As readers have often observed, the chasm visibly opens up between Jesus and his disciples in chapter 8, after the feeding of the 4000. They are on their way 'to the other side', to the pagan town of Bethsaida, and they have forgotten to bring sufficient food for the picnic. Jesus comments, 'Look! Watch out for the leaven of the Pharisees and the leaven of Herod', possibly referring to a recent brush with the Pharisees (8:11) who wanted 'a sign'. The disciples interpret this as a reference to their logistical failure, but Jesus is really criticising them for their failure to grasp the message of the two feeding stories, and ends the interrogation with, 'Do you not yet understand?' So a failure to grasp the mystery of Jesus is not something that has only recently happened to the Church, and it includes Jesus' closest associates.

From here on it seems that the painful division deepens. At 8:30 there is suddenly a great deal of 'rebuking' going on. Peter correctly identifies Jesus as 'the Messiah', but he and the rest of them are then 'rebuked', 'to say nothing to anybody about him'; at that point Jesus starts teaching them that the 'Son of Man has to suffer many things'. Peter cannot cope with this at all, but 'took hold of him and began to rebuke him'. Then in his turn Jesus 'saw the disciples and rebuked Peter, and says, "Get behind me, Satan – you are not thinking God-thoughts but human thoughts."'

This is the first of three 'Passion Predictions', after each of which the disciples make it clear that they have not been listening to a word he has been saying. The second prediction (9:30-2) is followed by an embarrassed silence when he asks them the innocent-sounding question: 'What were you arguing about on the road?', and it turns out that they had been discussing 'Who is Mr Big?'; and the third prediction (10:32-4) leads to James and John making a bid for power: 'Grant us to sit, one on your right and one on your left, in your glory' (10:37). This arouses the fury of the other ten, because James and John have got in there first.

There is more besides. At the Transfiguration, Peter (9:5, 6) ineptly responds with a suggestion of erecting a campsite for Jesus, Moses and Elijah; and Mark tartly comments that 'he did not know how he was to respond, for they had become terrified'. Later on, as they go down the mountain, there is another misunderstanding: 'What's this about being raised from the dead?' (9:10). Then at the bottom of the mountain, there is the man with a son who has an unclean spirit (9:17), and Jesus' disciples have proved not strong enough to expel the spirit. After Jesus has easily healed the boy, the disciples ask him, 'Why could we not expel it?' Once again Jesus towers way above them, as he does a few verses later (9:38), when the disciple John brightly tells him, 'Teacher, we saw someone casting out demons in your name, and we stopped him, because he was not one of our followers.' Jesus' response is good common sense, even if not absolutely obvious to John: 'Don't stop him, because no one who does a miracle in my name will speedily be able to bad-mouth me. For anyone who is not against us is on our side.' These disciples have much to learn, and the divisions are evident.

The divisions are evident again when it comes to the question of divorce (10:10-12), and children; the disciples think that Jesus is too important to be bothered with children, and Jesus' response is furious: 'Let the little children come to me; don't stop them' (10:14).

In a way, therefore, we are not surprised when at 14:10, 11 one of them actually offers to hand Jesus over to the High Priests. We have, of course, been told back at 3:19 that Judas was going to betray him, and here Mark emphasises that Judas is 'one of the Twelve' (14:10); however, it is worth noticing that when we get to the Last Supper they are all implicit in the betrayal of Jesus: 'one of you lot is going to betray me' (14:18), and then the horror deepens, 'one of the Twelve, the one who dips with me into the dish'. Then comes a second prediction of betrayal, for as they go into the Mount of Olives 'Jesus says to them, "you are all going to be made to fall away"' (14:27). In terrible contrast, Peter will have none of this: 'Even if they are all going to be made to fall, no way shall I be', and then, when Jesus predicts, 'You are going to deny me three times', he goes over the top: 'Even if I have to die with you, no way am I going to deny you.' And Mark comments: 'and they all said the same' (14:29-31). We know what is going to happen now, and the divisions between Jesus and his disciples are all too clear. It is no real surprise when Peter is (mildly) censured for sleeping at Jesus' moment of terror, when the three of them, Simon and the two sons of Zebedee, had been specifically asked to stay awake (14:32-7), nor when we come to that terrible moment of his arrest, when all those brave men, who had been promising they would never, ever deny Jesus, 'abandoned him and fled' (14:50), on the last train to Galilee.

Nor has the story of these divisions come to an end, even yet. For it turns out that Peter had not after all joined them in their panic-stricken exit, but 'he followed from a long way off', while Jesus is interrogated by the Sanhedrin (14:54). Then comes the saddest story of all, where Peter is terrorised by what Mark describes as 'just a single one of the little slave-girls of the High Priest', in contrast to Jesus' unruffled serenity and truth-telling, into noisily lying about Jesus: 'I neither know nor understand what you are talking about', and he does it twice more, culminating in the most terrible oath: 'He began to curse and swear, "I do not know this person whom you are talking about". And immediately the cock crowed a second time.' At that point, 'Peter remembered . . . and he broke down and wept' (14:66-71). And the reader is left wondering if it is now too late; are the divisions between Jesus and his disciples, especially Peter, beyond healing?

Mark has the most wonderful answer to this question, in the way that his Gospel ends; and we shall do well to remember it as we face the question of the divisions that so painfully exist between Christians today. For when the brave women go to the tomb on the Sunday morning, and meet a mysterious but knowledgeable young man, they are given instructions to 'go, and tell his disciples, *and Peter* that "he is going before you into the Galilee"' (16:7). Do you see what has happened here? The cowardice of the male disciples, and the terrible threefold denial of Peter, are healed and made better, and the divisions brought to an end.

Conclusion

So Mark's Gospel seems to have a good deal to say to us as we look at the painful problem of Christian divisions; for the evangelist presents us with a Jesus who is in various ways divided from the religious authorities of his culture and of his deeply loved religion, from his family and friends, and even from his own disciples. Those divisions, however, are not the end of the story; and nor need they be in our time and place, for Jesus is risen, and that means an end to all that human frailty can do.

CHAPTER 7

Divisions in Matthew's Gospel

In Matthew's Gospel, we see very much the pattern that we have encountered elsewhere in the New Testament: there are divisions – indeed, they are even expected – but they are not the end of the story. And yet we still need to recognise that Jesus is a divisive figure.

Joseph: a model for disciples

One happy Matthean innovation is the figure of Joseph. That is not to say that he is not mentioned in Mark; it is rather that Matthew does something quite interesting with him, which may serve as a model for us in dealing with the divisions that we find in the churches today. Joseph is a man who says nothing and just obeys, and perhaps we suffer from the dangerous temptation of always having to have something to say (or, you may wish to add, something to write!).

We meet him for the first time after his brief mention (1:16) in the genealogy of Jesus, at 1:18, where we learn that he is engaged to Mary, who has been found to be pregnant. This makes the situation extraordinarily tense, rich in potential division. Matthew tells us, first, that he is 'just', which is a very important idea in the first Gospel, and a high value. In this case his 'being just' consists in 'not wanting to make an example of her', so divorcing her without any fuss (but of course leaving her to the mercy of those who know what treatment to mete out to unmarried pregnant women); however, God intervenes, in the shape of an angel in a dream, and, giving him a full patronymic, tells him what to do: 'Joseph, son of David, don't be afraid to take Mary as your wife.' Matthew, as he will frequently do in this Gospel, then shows how this is a part of God's plan by saying, 'This whole thing happened in order that it might be fulfilled, what was spoken by the Lord through the prophet' (1:22). Then, to indicate how literally Joseph obeyed the instructions he had been given, he writes, 'Joseph arose from his sleep and did what the angel of the Lord had commanded him, and took his wife, and did not know her until she had borne a son. And he called his name "Jesus".' So a tricky situation is elegantly avoided, and in Joseph's silent and non-argumentative obedience there may be a way ahead for coping with our divisions.

We encounter the same pattern in the next chapter, after Matthew has related the story of the Magi, and to our relief diverted them back to their home territory 'by another route' (2:12). However, there remains a threat to the life of the newly born child, and so God has to intervene, using the same technique of an angel in a dream by night (2:13-15), and the instruction is followed by literal obedience:

> Arise and take the little child and its mother, and flee into Egypt, and be there until I tell you.

> [Joseph] arose and took the little child and its mother *by night*, and *went up* to Egypt. And he was there until the death of Herod.

Another of Matthew's 'scripture-fulfilment' sentences then follows this. For us, though, the point is that Joseph does exactly what he has been told. However, it is a bit subtler than that, for Matthew makes two small changes, which I have put in italics, between the instruction and the obedience, namely 'by night' and 'went up'. Both of these changes make a point about scripture-fulfilment: namely, in the first case, that we are meant to think of the Exodus, although of course that came from Egypt to Israel, not the other way around; and in the second case 'went up' is a verb that you normally use for going *to* Israel, not running *from* it. So Matthew has very delicately made two changes that underline the Old Testament background of this story: a Jewish king has rejected the Jewish Messiah, so the old story of the people of God must now be told in a different way. And it is only possible because one man is prepared, silently and without argument, to do what God tells him. There is something here for our living out the story of God's people.

Then comes a third dream for, at 2:19-21, we have the news of Herod's death, and then, 'Look! The angel of the Lord appears in a dream to Joseph in Egypt, saying, "Arise and take the little child and its mother and journey to the land of Israel"', and after that we are given the reason: 'for those who are seeking the little child's life have died'. Once more, Joseph shows literal obedience: 'He arose, and took the little child and its mother, and entered the land of Israel.' Here again there is an echo of the story of God's people, in the two phrases 'journey to the land of Israel' and 'entered the land of Israel'. This is the story as it should be, a new Exodus, which is only possible because Joseph has without argument done exactly what he was told to do.

Finally, Joseph responds to a fourth dream, which enables him to avoid Archelaus, who was at least as bloodthirsty as, but a great deal less competent than, his father, Herod the Great. Here we lose the pattern of command and obedience, and are simply told that 'he was afraid to go [to Judea]' and then that he was 'warned in a dream [and] he went up to the parts of the Galilee', so that once again Jesus is preserved from the bloody intentions of a Judean king, only because of the obedience of one man. And, once again, Matthew has a fulfilment-citation 'that it might be fulfilled what was spoken through the prophets, "he shall be called a Nazorean"'. So the power of destruction is avoided, and the child is preserved, because the God who is at work through the entire history of the people of God has intervened; but that intervention was only possible because one man was willing to be silently obedient. There is a clue here for handling our own contemporary divisions (2:22, 23).

Divisions in the Christian community

Matthew clearly expects that there will be divisions; so at 18:15-18, he offers no fewer than three ways of coping with tensions in the Church, or, as Jesus puts it, 'if your brother or sister sins against you'. First, 'you are to show them their fault, while you are alone with them'. Second, 'take one or two more people with you'; and, third, 'tell the church'. This passage recognises that these solutions may not work, and concludes, 'and if the person refuses to listen to the church, let them be like the tax collector and the Gentile to you'. That sounds like a firm exclusion; but then we might recall Jesus' subversive attitude to tax collectors like Matthew (9:9), and also the fact that the Gospel ends with Jesus telling his disciples to 'make disciples of all the Gentiles' (28:19). For our purposes, however, the point is clear: in Matthew's church a strategy was needed for dealing with divisions.

Indeed you might argue that much of chapter 18 envisages tensions of that kind. It starts with the question of 'Who is greatest in the Kingdom of the Heavens?' (18:1), and once you start asking who is really important, then you know that there is trouble on the way. Jesus' response would solve almost all of our dividedness: 'Summoning a little child, he set it in the middle of them, and said, "Amen I'm telling you, unless you people turn and become like little children, no way will you enter the Kingdom of the Heavens."' Once you understand this teaching, you are a great deal less likely to go in for silly squabbling; and Jesus continues with this theme, as he warns against 'scandalising one of these little ones who believes in me' and against 'despising these little ones'. For this purpose Matthew uses the story of the lost sheep, which in Luke's Gospel is told as an image of how God celebrates at the recovery of a single sinner.

The Unforgiving Servant

Best of all in this chapter is the parable often known as the Unforgiving Servant (18:23-35). One of the ways that we make our divisions worse is by taking ourselves too seriously; but this story does not take itself at all seriously, and may teach us the gift of laughing at ourselves when contemplating our being in the right. For it starts with Peter asking about forgiveness, possibly as a reaction to the instruction about what to do when the 'brother or sister sins against you' that we have just been looking at. Peter is scratching his head and wondering if there is a sensible upper limit to the number of times we are to forgive. He thinks of the biggest number in his computer and suggests 'as many as seven times?' Jesus multiplies this several times over: 'not as many as seven times; but as many as seventy times seven!' If you are calculating how long it will take you to get to 489, then you have missed the point. To make that point he tells a story at which we are supposed to laugh out loud. There are three characters: a king (think Roman emperor, if you like) and two slaves, as well as various others of that social status. The king (who is said to be 'like the Kingdom of the Heavens') is drawing up accounts, and then we meet Slave 1, who owes 10,000 talents. That is a simply immense sum, equivalent to the GNP of many a sizeable Greek city-state, and no king in his right mind would ever have allowed a debt of that size to mount up. At all events, this king is quite clear about his response, which is to sell the slave and his wife and children and all his possessions. The economically minded reader will be aware, however, that even this would be the merest drop in the ocean compared with the size of the debt.

Then the tone gets lighter, and we read (v.26) that 'the slave fell down and worshipped him [which in Matthew's Gospel is something that you can only do to Jesus or God], saying, "Be patient with me and I shall repay you the whole lot."' This is high comedy, for there are no circumstances under which a slave could possibly lay his hands on a sum of this sort, as Matthew's hearers well knew. Then, to our astonishment, we see a different side of the king; for quite unexpectedly he 'was gutted and set him free and remitted him the debt'.

That unexpected turn of events, however, is only the platform for further comedy. For now we watch the next episode, as 'that slave went out and found one of his fellow slaves [Slave 2] who owed him a hundred denarii'. Now a denarius is often taken to be a day's wage, because that is the currency in the parable of the workers in the vineyard (Matthew 20:2); but the Roman legionaries only got 225 denarii a year, so the debt may have been half a year's wages; but at all events it bears no comparison to 10,000 talents. The comedy continues, as Slave 1 'grabbed him and strangled him' (in stark contrast to the treatment that Slave 1 has just received from the king!), 'saying, "Pay back what you owe."' Then Slave 2 uses exactly the same phrase that we have heard Slave 1 addressing to the king: 'Be patient with me and I shall give it back to you.' As we listen, we reflect that he has a much better chance of repaying 100 denarii than Slave 1 has of repaying 10,000 talents.

The absurdity continues, as Slave 1 'went off and flung him into prison until he should pay what was owed'. Then the other slaves get in on the act and tell the king what has been going on; and finally the king gives his verdict: 'You wicked slave, I let you off all that debt, because you begged me. Should you not have mercied your fellow slave, as I mercied you?' (and the reader will remember here the words of the Beatitude at Matthew 5:7: 'Congratulations to the merciful, for they shall be mercied'). Sentence is passed: 'And the king in a rage handed him over to the torturers until he should pay back the whole lot of what was owed.' Now it is a scientifically proven fact that no amount of torture will ever expand one's bank balance, certainly not to the extent of 10,000 talents, and clearly we are not meant to take it seriously, still less the horrifying coda: 'So my Father, the Heavenly One, will do to you, unless you each forgive your brother or sister from your hearts.' We need to laugh, and ruefully acknowledge our over-serious concentration on our debts.

Some very challenging teaching

One of the things that we have frequently noticed in this book is that Jesus is a divisive figure. Matthew does not hide from this fact, and offers us some very challenging teaching.

The Sermon on the Mount

This is particularly evident in the Sermon on the Mount (chapters 5–7).

Matthew sets the scene with some care. 'Seeing the crowd, he went up in to the mountain', and the impression that we get is that he is in flight from the crowd, that this teaching is just for 'the disciples' (5:1); however, Matthew corrects that notion, and at the end of the Sermon (7:28, 29) it is the crowds, rather than the disciples, who were 'amazed at his teaching'.

Nevertheless, we have a sense that this somewhat rarefied teaching may be just for the few, for the phrase that Matthew uses – 'went up into the mountain' – is exactly what the Greek translation of the Old Testament says about Moses (look at Exodus 19:3). The point here is that Jesus is presented as a new (and better) Moses, which is itself divisive.

Then the shocks continue apace, as Jesus '*opened his mouth*, and *began to teach* them, *saying*', and these three words of speaking have us focused very attentively on what it is that Jesus is about to say. And what he says is very challenging indeed, a series of 'congratulations' to all the wrong sorts of people: 'the destitute in spirit, those who mourn, the meek(!), those who hunger and thirst for justice, the merciful, the pure in heart, the peace-makers and those who are persecuted for the sake of justice'. This is not what is normally said in fashionable religious and political discourse; but that may be because such discourse does not always recognise the challenging, not to say subversive, phenomenon that is the Sermon on the Mount.

What holds chapters 5 to 7 together is nothing other than the dangerous radicalism of the view (shared by Pope Francis) that God is our Father. If you look carefully at these three chapters, you will see that the Lord's Prayer comes right in the middle of them, and that Matthew has constructed it thus; for into the teaching on almsgiving, prayer and fasting, where the basic line is 'do it discreetly, where only your heavenly Father can see you', Matthew has inserted the Prayer, and that is what holds the entire Sermon together.

That is how we are to understand the undeniably divisive-sounding teachings of these chapters. For example, at 5:17-20, we hear Matthew's church facing the challenge of the 'synagogue across the road'; they have evidently been arguing that Matthew's church has sold the pass with regard to observance of the Law of Moses, and Matthew has Jesus insist that:

I have not come to destroy but to fulfil [the Law and the Prophets]. For Amen I am telling you, until heaven and earth pass away, not a single iota nor a single serif is going to pass away from the Law, until everything happens.

Then it gets a bit heated:

For I am telling you that unless your righteousness overflows more than the scribes and Pharisees, no way will you enter the Kingdom of the Heavens.

You can feel the divisions here; and then there is the alarming prohibition (5:22) against calling a brother [or sister] 'Raka' or 'Fool'; but of course that is intended to mitigate the divisions. We might also reflect that the passion here is nothing compared with the shrill tone of contemporary bloggers, even those who affect to be religiously minded. When at 5:45 we read the invitation to become 'children of your Father, the one in the heavens, because he makes his sun rise on wicked and good and rains upon just and unjust', we can substitute there 'on Protestants and Catholics' for a sobering comment on our contemporary divisions.

In the Sermon there is constant reference to 'hypocrites' (6:2, 5, 16, for example), which is simply the Greek word for 'actors', and is a charge that is often laid with justice against us who are of a religious disposition. The clue here, once more, is the centrality of the Lord's Prayer, which is precisely not a matter of acting, but of 'telling it how it is'.

And we must be ready to laugh at ourselves. At 7:3-5 Jesus tells us of the comic absurdity of how you and I react in religious dialogue, with the picture of me offering to take a splinter out of your eye, while I have an enormous plank of wood in my own. You may be able to think of similar examples in your own experience of inter-religious dialogue; but concentrate on examples that turn the laugh on yourself or on your own religious tradition, if you want to get the point.

Then at 7:12, Jesus gives us what is often called the 'Golden Rule': 'Everything that you want people to do to you, you are to behave like that to them. For this is the Law and the Prophets.' This, then, is to be the test for what we say about each other: have you ever said 'X' about a fellow Christian?

Divisions elsewhere in the Gospel

Even outside the Sermon on the Mount there is challenging teaching; of all people, a Gentile centurion approaches Jesus (8:5-13), asking for healing for his son or slave (the Greek word could mean either), and insisting that, instead of coming to his unworthy establishment, Jesus simply give orders to the disease, and the child/slave will be cured immediately. Listen, however, to Jesus' comment on what the centurion says (8:10-12):

> Jesus was astonished and said to his followers, 'Amen I am telling you: nowhere in Israel have I found faith like this. But I am telling you: many are going to come from East and West and will lie down with Abraham and Isaac and Jacob in the kingdom of the heavens; while the children of the kingdom are going to be expelled into the outer darkness.'

This is exceptionally strong language, the more so given that Matthew is ordinarily thought to be a very Jewish Gospel. This is not a Gospel for weaklings.

At the same time, Jewish people are not simply dismissed. They are made the prime targets of the mission of the Twelve in chapter 10, when Jesus' emissaries are instructed not to 'go off on the road to the Gentiles, and not to go into a city of Samaritans; but go, rather, to the lost sheep of the house of Israel' (vv.5, 6). So the mission is still aimed at God's holy people; and we can guess that for some in Matthew's church this will have been hard to swallow.

The divisive person of Jesus

The fact is that the Jesus of Matthew's Gospel is very divisive. Consider the following remarks:

> 'Do not think that I came to throw peace on the earth. I did not come to throw peace, but a sword! For I came to divide "a man against his father, and a daughter against her mother, and a bride against her mother-in-law; and a person's enemies are those of his own household"' (10:34-6).

The last sentence is a citation of Micah 7:6; but that does not take away the sharply divisive tone. There is even a hint of tension with his forerunner, John the Baptist, who sends from prison to ask, 'Are you the Coming One, or are we to wait for another?' The message that is returned is quite sharp: 'Congratulations to the one who is not made to stumble with regard to me' (11:3, 6). However, the next verses make it clear that Jesus and John are basically on the same side, and the division is sketched between Jesus and John on the one hand, and their Palestinian audience on the other. These last are likened to children, 'who sit in the market-place and address each other:

'We played the pipes for you, and you didn't dance;
we played mourning-tunes, and you didn't weep' (11:16, 17).

Jesus continues with the reflection that John the Baptist was rejected because his austerity gave rise to the verdict that 'he has a demon', while Jesus was rejected because 'he is a glutton and a wine-drinker, a friend of tax-collectors and sinners'. We form the image of one who can please nobody, but simply causes divisions.

What is to be done about divisions in the Church? Matthew offers what you might call a principle of unity against division, when he tells the story at 16:13-20 of Peter's declaration at Caesarea Philippi. Here Peter proclaims (perfectly correctly) that Jesus is 'the Messiah, the Son of the Living God'. In response, Jesus congratulates him, on the grounds that the source of this revelation is 'not flesh and blood, but my Father, the one in the heavens'. Then he offers the source of unity: 'And I am telling you, that you are Rock and on this rock I am going to build my church [or 'assembly'] and the gates of Hades will not be strong against it.' Now it is perfectly true that Peter immediately goes to the bottom of the class with his refusal to accept that Jesus is going to 'suffer many things from the elders and chief priests and scribes and be killed and on the third day be raised'; nevertheless, according to this story, that Christological confession is the basis on which we are to contest all disunion in the Church.

Some of Jesus' parables, especially as we get near to the end of the Gospel, give us a graphic picture of the disunity. For example, the story of the Labourers in the Vineyard (Matthew 20:1-16), where the workers who were first to be employed, instead of showing gratitude to the master of the household for having given them a job, complain at the end of the day because they have only been given the sum that they agreed, and argue that 'we bore the heat and burden of the day', and should have been paid more than 'these latecomers [who] did one hour'. The story is set up for its climax by the odd decision (v.8) to 'begin [making the payment] with the latecomers, down to the first', which focuses the reader's attention on their complaints. Their eyes are on themselves, not on God.

The same is true of the parable of the Wedding Feast (22:1-13), which Matthew places immediately after that other vineyard parable, that of the Tenants (21:33-46). By this time it has become clear that Jesus and the religious authorities are divided beyond the possibility of reconciliation. In this context, the parable is decidedly belligerent: those invited to the wedding feast make implausible and discourteous responses, so others are invited in their place. Notice, however, that the story does not end there, but with one of the latest set of invitees, who, although he has attended, is wearing the wrong clothes. The warning here is that it is possible, even for those who benefit from God's generosity, to exclude oneself from God's offer by way of various kinds of wrong attitude and self-exclusion. We cannot but read this in the context of the division between Jesus and the various religious authorities (High Priests and Pharisees, 21:45; Pharisees with Herodians, 22:15, 16; Sadducees, 22:23; Pharisees on their own, 22:34, 41) and recognise that the way to put our divisions right is to keep our eyes on God and on Jesus.

And that is the secret for understanding the otherwise very uncomfortable discourse against the 'scribes and Pharisees' (23:1-38) – that the religious authorities have precisely not kept their eyes on God. We have to read this as an inter-Jewish controversy, with its seven 'woes', which are still applicable to religious authorities today, especially when we fail to recognise that 'you have just one Teacher, and you are all brothers and sisters ... you have one Father, the Heavenly One' (23:8, 9). It is the failure to recognise this important truth that brings about divisions in religious groups.

We should also notice that religious groups can all too often make extravagant claims, especially about what God is going to do next: 'The world will end on 23 January in the year 20XX', if uttered with sufficient confidence, can inspire credence among followers of a particular group; and Jesus warns against precisely such false claims in religious discourse at 24:4-11: '... people saying, "I am the Messiah" ... many false prophets shall arise and lead many people astray'. Being religious is no protection against leading others into disaster.

Divisive episodes in Matthew

There are plenty of episodes in the first Gospel that reveal the author's expectation that divisions will ensue. So at 1:19 we discover that Joseph is 'just', but reluctant to have a public divorce. This would have been shocking for many of his co-religionists, while the reader is well aware that if he had indeed put Mary away 'privately', the whole story would have ground to a halt. Or consider the effect of John the Baptist's challenge to 'Pharisees and Sadducees' at 3:7-12, which we are presumably intended to applaud: 'brood of vipers', he roundly addresses them, 'who warned you to flee from the wrath that is about to be?', before going on to focus on 'the one coming after me, who is stronger than me, and I am not fit to carry his sandals'. That is how we are to cope with our divisions. Another model is to be found in the verses immediately following, the 'spat' between John the Baptist and Jesus, where each is trying to outdo the other in courtesy: that is how Christians are to behave in their dealings with each other.

Or consider Matthew's version of the temptations of Jesus (4:1-11), where the one known as 'the devil' or 'the Tempter' outlines his normal strategy of causing division by making seductively attractive suggestions to Jesus about making a grab for his status as 'Son of God'. Jesus, by contrast, models non-divisive behaviour, by refusing to use his skills to acquire food and followers, or to worship anything but God.

Then at the other end of the Gospel, in chapter 25 we are offered no fewer than three parables on unity which do their work by focusing on Jesus, not on ourselves: that of the Ten Virgins (1-13), where the difference is between those who were and those who were not ready for Jesus' coming; that of the Talents (14-30), where the point is the need for a generous response to the Lord's generosity; and, finally, 31-46 (the Sheep and the Goats), challenging us to see Christ in the unexpected guise of the poor and needy.

A final divisive episode comes at 27:62-6, 28:11-15, which is the story of the guards placed over the tomb by, once more, the 'High Priests and Pharisees' (27:62), to make sure that there is no nonsense about Resurrection after Jesus' death. The stratagem fails, because an angel rolls the stone away (28:2), and those who are supposed to be guarding a corpse themselves become 'like corpses' (28:4); when they carry their rueful report to the High Priests, their response is bribery and lies, which of course only serves to verify the claim that Jesus' tomb was empty on that Sunday morning. So our task is to keep our gaze on the God who raised Jesus from the dead, and that will mean an end of all our divisions.

Conclusion

So at the end of our tour through the first Gospel, we see that, despite everything, divisions are not the problem; divisions are only to be expected, and the problem lies in how we handle them, where we put our energy, and where our gaze is focused. If we want to avoid divisions, then the focus has to be on God and on Jesus. Our model in coping with all this is the silently obedient figure of Joseph.

CHAPTER 8

Divisions in Luke's Gospel

Introduction: the silence of Mary

We ended the previous chapter by speaking of Joseph's obedient silence as a model for coping with divisions in Matthew's Gospel. We turn now to the Gospel of Luke, and here we find that it is Mary's silence that functions as a model for the reader. In truth, she says very little, and this may be a model for all of us in situations of division. We meet her first at the Annunciation (Luke 1:26-38), where she only actually speaks twice. On the first occasion (v.34), she asks the sensible question, 'How will this be, since I do not know a man?'; then, as we hang on her words, she gives her answer to Gabriel: 'Look – the Lord's slave-girl' (v.38), which is all that any of us needs to say.

The next time we hear her speak, it is the Magnificat (1:46-55), with its emphasis on the importance of the unimportant: 'He looked on the humiliation of his slave-girl' (v.48); 'he scattered the arrogant in the thoughts of their heart' (v.51); 'he took down the rulers from their thrones', 'he raised up the humbled' (v.52); 'he sent the rich away empty' (v.53). Her next speech (and her only remaining one in the entire Gospel) is a reproach to her adolescent son: 'Child – why have you treated us like this? Your father and I have been in agony looking for you', which leads to a tutorial on the meaning of the word 'Father' (2:48, 49), which Mary does not immediately understand.

However, we also need to notice the two or three important things that she does in the story. First, in the light of the annunciation from Gabriel, she sets off on the daunting journey, apparently quite alone, from Nazareth to the Judean hill country, where she meets Elisabeth and is told more of the identity of her unborn child (1:39-45). Then come two key moments, at which Luke is clearly making her a model. First, after the shepherds have come and gone, and made their revelation about what the Lord (2:15) had made known to them, Luke comments that 'Mary was keeping these things/words, considering them in her heart'. Then after the episode of Jesus lost and found in the Temple, he writes 'and his mother was keeping all these words/things in her heart' (2:51b). This silent reflection is not a bad way of dealing with our divisions.

The unimportance of the important

Another good way of coping with divisions is to recognise that we may often be wrong about what and who is really important. At the beginning of each of his first three chapters Luke plays what you might call 'the three-card trick', showing us those who appear to be most important before revealing that they are not at all the people in whom he is interested. For he makes us look first at the powerful of this world, before making the reader aware that this is not the way God sees things.

So at 1:5 we read, just like the opening of a history of the mighty, 'It happened in the days of Herod the king of Judea ...'. Then, just as you feel you are settling down for some good Greek history, Luke takes you by surprise and introduces you to a priestly family: 'a certain priest called Zachariah, from the ephemery of Abijah, and his wife, of the daughters of Aaron – and her name was Elisabeth'. Luke's cultivated readers may have been expected to know the meaning of the names of this charming Old Testament couple: 'The Lord has remembered' and 'My God has sworn an oath' (and of the son who has yet to be born to them, and is to be called 'John', a name which means 'the Lord has acted graciously'); and the point for the reader is that Luke has no interest at all in Herod, and wants us to keep our eyes on what God is doing in these relatively unimportant persons, who are going to be an early step in God's new project.

Luke repeats this trick at the beginning of the next chapter (2:1-5), when he invites us to contemplate the most powerful man in the world, 'Caesar Augustus', who sends out a 'decree' to 'the whole world' that they were all to be written down in a record; and Luke also mentions the second most important person in Palestine, namely Quirinius, who had risen rapidly on the Roman ladder of promotion, and had close relations with Caesar's family, and who, Luke tells us, carried out a census of the people (a procedure which is discouraged at least once in the Old Testament; see 2 Samuel 24:1-10; 1 Chronicles 24:1-5). However, it is neither of these high-ups that catches Luke's interest, in this episode where 'everyone was going off to be registered, to their own city'. Instead, his camera focuses on 'Joseph from Galilee, of the city of Nazareth ... with Mary his fiancée – who was pregnant'. Then we watch attentively as 'the days were fulfilled' (a sure sign that God is at work) 'for her to give birth' and she placed her newborn son in a 'feeding-trough' (think of a 'dog-bowl'). Again, it is the unimportant to whom we are invited to give importance. That is, we shall see, a good way to deal with our divisions.

Then Luke performs the same trick again at the beginning of his third chapter (3:1, 2). Here we have left behind the childhood of both Jesus and John the Baptist, and stand on the verge (as it turns out) of Jesus' ministry. Once again the focus is on the important (and perhaps rather unsavoury) of this world, as we encounter the only date in the entire New Testament:

> In the fifteenth year of the imperium of Tiberius Caesar,
> when Pontius Pilate was procurator of Judea,
> and Herod was tetrarch of Galilee
> and Philip his brother was tetrarch of the Iturea and Trachonitis region
> and Lysanius was tetrarch of Abilene [there may be some confusion over
> the historical details here]
> in the priesthood of Hannas and Caiaphas,
> the word of God came to . . .

The date is roughly AD29, and once again Luke has mentioned the People Who Count in the world in which his Gospel is going to be played out, Syria-Palestine in the first third of the first century; and the people who count are, taken all in all, a pretty disreputable bunch. It is, however, to none of these that Luke mentions God's word being addressed; instead it comes 'to John the son of Zachariah'. And where is this privileged recipient of the divine utterance to be found? Where Luke had placed him, back in verse 80 of chapter 1: 'in the desert, until the day of his showing to Israel' (compare 3:2), from which now he comes proclaiming, not the salvific power of the emperor of Rome, but a very different message – 'baptism of repentance for the forgiveness of sins'. There is a very important message here when it comes to considering our divisions.

The offensive language of religious discourse

One of the things that happen in debates between persons of different religions, or those of different branches of the same religion, is that they use the most dreadfully offensive language of each other. This is something that we certainly need to keep under control, for words can do the most terrible damage. John the Baptist, it has to be said, does not give us a very good example at 3:7, 8:

> To the crowds who came out to be baptised by him, he said, 'Brood of vipers! Who showed you to flee from the wrath that is coming? So produce fruits worthy of repentance, and don't start saying inside yourselves, "We have Abraham as a father."'

Luke invites us to applaud this rant, but we need to bear in mind its possible consequences. Later on in the Gospel, and this time we are clearly not invited to applaud, James and John (whom, according to Mark 3:17, Jesus nicknamed 'sons of thunder', possibly because of outbursts like this) made the following explosive intervention (9:51-5):

It happened when the days of his taking-up were being fulfilled, and he himself set his face to journey to Jerusalem. And he sent messengers before his face; and they journeyed and entered a village of the Samaritans, to make ready for him. And they did not give him hospitality, because his face was journeying to Jerusalem. And seeing this, the disciples James and John said, 'Lord, do you want us to tell fire to come down from heaven and consume them?' But he turned and rebuked them.

In the history of religion, many sincere believers have felt moved to violence of this sort, and many religions remain beset with divisions that have been put in place by precisely this sort of violence. Christians have not been exempt from this; and the next time we feel tempted in this way, we should go back to this passage, and read once more Jesus' reaction to the explosive sons of Zebedee. It can seem so tempting to kill off the enemies of our religion; but this is not the Christian way.

Opponents who use offensive language

Quite often, of course, it is our opponents who use the violent language. This is what takes place in the story of what we might call the 'Good Samaritan and the Bad Lawyer' (10:25-37). Here a lawyer (who is out to get Jesus) asks him the potentially lethal question, 'What am I to do, teacher, to inherit eternal life?' Jesus throws the ball back to him, asking what the Law says (he is a professional, after all), and elicits the double commandment: love God, and love your neighbour. For Jesus that is the end of the question. The lawyer is still closing in on his target, however (as religious people at our worst can tend to do), and, 'wishing to justify himself, said to Jesus, "So who is my 'neighbour'?"' Then comes a most unexpected interlude, for Jesus (as so often, it must be said, especially in Luke's Gospel) tells a story, the one we know as the Good Samaritan, contrasting the unwelcome foreigner with the two religious professionals. They circled round the man who had been mugged, while he went straight in to help. At the end of the story, which is remarkably detailed, Jesus turns to his aggressive interlocutor and asks, 'Which of these three men, in your opinion, became a "neighbour" to the one who fell among muggers?' The answer is not nearly so detailed, and the lawyer cannot bring himself to mention the name of the unwelcome foreigner, and says, simply, 'The one who did the act of mercy on him'. To this, Jesus brings the conversation to an end with the remark, 'On your way – and you are to do just the same.' This is a very unexpected way of defusing the tension that offensive religious discourse can produce.

One example of such discourse is the statement often found on the lips of religious people that people's suffering is their own fault – it is because they have sinned. In Luke's Gospel, we find that issue approached when Jesus is asked about an article in that day's newspaper 'about the Galileans whose blood Pilate mixed with their sacrifices' (13:1-5). We know nothing of this story, except that, from what we know of Pontius Pilate, we should not be surprised to learn that he had behaved in this way, presumably murdering some Galilean pilgrims, on some pretext or other, and doing something to show his contempt for their rituals. At the same time, of course, the reader is aware that Jesus is a Galilean, and that Pilate is shortly going to shed his blood also. So the conversation could be read as an invitation to Jesus to use offensive religious language. Jesus will have none of it, however, and instead makes it an invitation to them to repent, 'or you'll die in the same way'. Then he takes another piece from the news, about the skyscraper at Siloam that fell on 18 people and killed them, and once again, rather than using offensive language, turns the story into one about the need for his hearers to repent.

Another piece of offensive religious discourse occurs when Jesus heals a woman on the Sabbath (13:10-17). Luke wins our sympathy by revealing that the woman had had 'a spirit of sickness for 18 years, and was bent over and unable to straighten up at all', and Jesus authoritatively tells her 'you are freed from your sickness' and then 'he laid his hands on her. And right away she was straightened up and she glorified God.' So we know what side we are on. However, then we meet the 'ruler of the synagogue', and learn that he is 'annoyed because Jesus had healed on the Sabbath'. He does not attack Jesus directly (and you may think this characteristic of those who use offensive religious discourse); instead it is the crowd whom he berates: 'There are six days on which people must work. So come and be healed on those days, and not on the Sabbath day.' Jesus talks directly to him, and sharply accuses him of hypocrisy: 'Any one of you, on the Sabbath, unties his cow or donkey from the trough and leads them to have a drink.' Then he makes the contrast with the offensive discourse: 'But this woman, who is a daughter of Abraham, whom Satan had held bound, look! for 18 years; should she not have been untied from this shackle, on the Sabbath day?' Then Luke gives us the crowd's reaction: 'When he said this, all his opponents were put to shame before him. And the entire crowd was rejoicing at all the glorious things that were done by him.' The offensive discourse is neutralised, and there may be a model for us here.

The final instance under this heading comes towards the end of this same chapter (13:31-3), when 'some Pharisees' try to get him away 'because Herod wants to kill you'. It is hard to tell whether they are genuinely seeking Jesus' interests, or seeking to distract him from his journey to Jerusalem. In the end, it is not Herod but Pilate who will succeed in killing Jesus, though, as we shall see, Herod does appear in Luke's narrative of Jesus' last days. There is, however, no doubt about the force of Jesus' remark about Herod: 'Go and tell that fox that today and tomorrow and the next day I am expelling demons and completing healings. However, today and tomorrow and the next day I must journey onwards – for it is not acceptable for a prophet to die outside Jerusalem.' Is this offensive discourse? Certainly he is on the way to death.

The need for generous speech

One thing that is absolutely necessary is that we learn to speak generously of each other, across our divisions. John the Baptist offers us a good model of such speech in what he says about Jesus (3:16-18). Instead of seeing Jesus as his rival, he describes him in very generous terms: 'the one stronger than me, and I am not worthy to untie the thong of his sandals. He himself is going to baptise you in the Holy Spirit and with fire.' Jesus does the same, in the extraordinary chapter 15, a collection of three stories which starts and ends with the ungenerosity of opponents.

What holds chapter 15 together is the grudging reaction of those who cannot cope with God's mercy. It starts with 'tax collectors and sinners drawing near to listen to him', and 'muttering' or 'grumbling' on the part of 'the Pharisees and the scribes' because 'this one gives hospitality to sinners, and eats with them'. This is, alas, a common enough reaction among good religious people who tend to think that God is, or should be, interested only in good religious people. So Jesus tells three utterly subversive stories about God throwing a party in celebration at rediscovering the lost. There is a man's story: that of the shepherd who abandons the 99 sheep and goes in search of the missing one (vv.3-7); then there is a woman's story, of the lady who loses one drachma out of the miserable ten that is all her husband allows her for housekeeping, and who throws a party that in all probability cost more than a drachma to celebrate (vv.8-10). Finally, there is the story of a parent, utterly besotted with love for his appalling sons, so much so that when the younger son demands the portion that is coming to him in the old man's will, he 'divided his life between them' (vv.11-32). Not only that, but when the younger son is driven home by no more edifying motive than that of hunger, the parent is out there with his binoculars, looking for the boy's return, and then he covers him with kisses! The story does not end there, however, but rejoins at its end the ungenerosity of Jesus' opponents. The narrator manages this in the person of the 'elder brother', who comes in from working in the fields and refuses to join the party. As with his sibling, the father comes out to him and 'begged him'. The elder brother makes quite a good argument, that he has been 'slaving for you, and I never transgressed any commandment of yours; and you never even gave me a he-goat to have a party with my friends'. The father's point – and if we find it uncomfortable, we too may be in danger of being small-minded and divisive – is simply that when people come back, it is time to throw a party. With some skill, the evangelist does not tell us how the elder brother reacted to the challenge; the reason for that is that it is up to the reader (or hearer) to decide whether or not they buy into the generosity of God: will you, O Reader, opt to go in and join the party? Or not?

The final example of generous speech comes in an entirely unexpected conversation, right at the end of Jesus' life (Luke 23:39-43). The setting is that Jesus is hanging on the cross, and has asked, 'Father, forgive them' (23:34, though it is not in all manuscripts). The people 'stood, contemplating'; but the rulers 'sneered' (v.35) and the soldiers 'mocked' (v.36), inviting him to 'save [him]self'. It is all of a piece with this that 'one of the evil-doers hanging with him reviled him' and repeated and elaborated the invitation, 'Save yourself – and us too!' Then, to our astonishment, we get the first generous utterance. It comes from 'the other one'. This character reproves his accomplice, 'Do you have no fear of God, because you are under the same sentence, and we have deserved it . . . but this one has done nothing out of place' (vv.40, 41). Remarkably, and quite understandably, he then says, 'Jesus – remember me, when you come into your kingdom' (v.42). This generosity is matched by even greater generosity on Jesus' part, when, in magisterial, even regal, tones, he utters his response: 'Amen I'm telling you – today you are going to be with me in paradise.' This is a different level of conversation altogether.

Jesus a divisive figure, destined to die

The fact is, and this will come as no surprise to the alert reader of this book, that Jesus is a divisive figure, one who is from the beginning likely to die, and whose followers may well have the same fate coming to them.

Almost at the beginning of his ministry Luke makes this point with a story, that of the visit to the synagogue in Nazareth, which he found in Mark's Gospel at a much later point, and puts it right at the beginning of Jesus' ministry (4:14-30), so that it functions like a sort of mission statement. He is invited to read from the Isaiah scroll, and 'found the place where it was written "The Spirit of the Lord upon me . . . good news to the poor . . . freedom for prisoners . . . sight to the blind"'. The audience is hanging on his words, but Jesus is not afraid to be provocative: 'no prophet is acceptable in his own country', and he gives the examples of those daunting Galilean 'men of God', Elijah and Elisha, with the result that 'everyone in the synagogue was filled with rage when they heard this, and they got up and threw him outside the city, and led him to the brow of the mountain on which their city was built, so as to throw him down a cliff'. For the moment, Jesus escapes: 'He went through the middle of them and journeyed on'. But the writing, as the prophet Daniel remarked, is on the wall.

Luke's 'disastrous dinner-parties'

Another point at which the divisiveness of Jesus appears in the third Gospel is an area that you might call 'divisions at the dinner-table', or 'Luke's disastrous dinner-parties'. Here we shall mention just four of them. The first is the anointing of Jesus' feet by a woman (7:36-50), a story that the other three evangelists relate just before Jesus' passion. Luke, however, has taken it from that moment and made it a story about love and forgiveness. For our purposes, the point is that Jesus divides opinion. In this instance we notice the odd fact that it is a Pharisee who has invited Jesus to dine with him; into this potentially slightly hostile audience there erupts a woman, who treats him very intimately indeed, weeping over his feet, and kissing them and wiping them with the hair of her head. The Pharisee makes the shocked private comment that 'if this one were a prophet, he would have known who is this woman who is touching him, and what kind of a person she is – she is a sinner'. Jesus responds by refusing to retreat an inch, and tells his host a parable about love, the woman's demonstration of it, and his host's failure. At the end, and to the consternation of his fellow diners, he says to the woman: 'Your sins are forgiven', and then, 'your faith has saved you; off you go in peace.'

Our second 'disastrous dinner-party' is again in a Pharisee's house (11:37-54), and death is on the agenda. This one is a breakfast-party, at which his host expresses astonishment that Jesus does not do the proper ritual washing. Jesus responds with some vigour: 'Woe to you Pharisees! You love the front bench in synagogues and respectful greetings in the public forum.' When a lawyer intervenes in the debate, he gets the same treatment: 'Woe to you lawyers also!' Without going into the precise nature of the disagreement, we may notice, first, the high degree of tension here, and second, the upshot: 'When he went out, the scribes and the Pharisees started to express their hostility towards him, and to get him to talk about more things, setting an ambush for him, to snare him from his own mouth.'

The third and worst of these episodes is at 14:1-24. Here we are at the 'house of one of the rulers of the Pharisees, on the Sabbath [and we know that always means trouble], to eat a meal'. Then comes a very telling comment: 'and they were watching him carefully'. Into this tense scene Luke introduces 'a certain man with dropsy', and Jesus takes the fight to them: 'Is it permissible to heal on the Sabbath or not?' As they make no answer, Jesus simply heals the man (as though it were the most natural thing in the world), and takes the controversy to them: 'Which of you, if your son or your ox falls into a well, will not immediately drag him out on the Sabbath day?' Then it gets worse, and Jesus attacks his fellow guests for wanting the best places, and his host for only inviting the Right Sort of People. Someone else now intervenes, possibly trying to restore a measure of calm to the party, which is now in pieces, and utters the pious sentiment: 'Happy is the one who eats food in the kingdom of God.' This unexceptionable utterance provokes Jesus to the story of the Great Banquet, and the excuses made by those who had been invited, and the man's extension of the invitation to 'the poor, and the crippled and the lame and the blind', and finally to absolutely everybody: 'compel them to come in, that my house may be full', and the retraction of the invitation to the first potential guests: 'none of those men will taste my supper'.

Our final example under this heading is neither disastrous nor a dinner-party, and it comes at 19:1-10, the episode of Zacchaeus, when the journey has almost reached Jerusalem. Unexpectedly, perhaps, our sympathy is with Zacchaeus, despite the fact that he is 'a chief tax collector and rich' (v.2). The reason for this is that 'he sought to see who Jesus was', so we know that he is on the right side. Then, secondly, we learn that he was 'vertically challenged' (v.3), and so, once again, our sympathy is with him. This goes deeper as we watch him 'running ahead' and climbing a sycamore tree (v.4). Now he is trapped in the branches as this religious figure points up at him, and calls his name: 'Zacchaeus!' He must feel very exposed, but what happens next is not at all what he would have expected: 'Hurry up and come down, for today I must stay in your house' (v.5). Zacchaeus' response confirms our instinct: 'He hurried up and came down [literal obedience, you see] and joyfully gave him hospitality' (v.6). Then the divisions become evident: 'They all muttered, saying, "he has gone in to lodge with a sinner man."' And Zacchaeus comes out strikingly on the right side: he addresses Jesus as 'Lord', for one thing; and for another he makes startling restitution: 'I am giving half of my possessions to the poor, and if I have extorted from anybody [which as a chief tax collector he had almost certainly done] I am giving it back *fourfold*' (v.8). Jesus' comment completes the picture: 'Today, salvation has come to this house. For the Son of Man came to seek and to save what had been lost.' This is not a popular doctrine, and it will divide Jesus from those who know what religious figures should be like.

Other examples of Jesus' divisiveness

Luke includes some other episodes where Jesus is a source of division, which cannot properly be called 'disastrous dinner-parties' (though I have occasionally tried to include some of them under this rubric). The first one is what you might call 'on helping at home', though that title does not really capture what the story is about. It is the tale of Jesus' visit to Martha and Mary, on his great journey to Jerusalem (10:38-42). It is an odd story, since the principal character is a woman, and we notice with pleasure that 'Martha gave him hospitality' (v.38), which is a high value in the third Gospel. However, the narrator's focus then goes to her sister, who does not actually do anything except 'sit at the feet of the Lord, listening to his word'. Martha by contrast is doing far too much, 'she is torn apart by much service', and adopts a minatory posture: 'she stood over him' and says in an aggressive tone: 'Lord – don't you care that my sister [like the lawyer earlier in the chapter, she is too angry to mention her name] has abandoned me to serve alone? So tell her to help me!' Jesus' response must soften all division: 'Martha, Martha,' he says, the repetition of her name contrasting with her refusal to name Mary, and taking the sting from any implied criticism, and finally giving a narrow judgement in favour of Mary: 'she has chosen the better part, which is not going to be taken away from her.' Significantly perhaps, this story is placed between that of the lawyer that led to the tale of the Good Samaritan (10:25-37) and the disciples' request for a lesson in prayer that yielded Luke's version of what we call 'the Lord's Prayer' (11:1-4).

This story was perhaps a story of a division healed; but Luke is well aware that Jesus can be the source of division. Consider the remarks at 12:49-53: 'I came to throw fire on the earth . . . do you think that I came to give peace in the land? No, I'm telling you, but division!', followed by a list of the family ties where the division would be felt: 'father against son and son against father, mother against daughter and daughter against mother; mother-in-law against daughter-in-law' [there are of course those who would argue that this last division does not require divine intervention to maintain it or bring it about]. This is not, you see, 'gentle Jesus, meek and mild'.

The same tone reappears at 14:25, 26, when Jesus tells the crowd, 'If someone comes to me and does not hate their father and mother and wife and children and brothers and sisters, yes, and their own life, they cannot be my disciple.' This is a stark message, and gives a context to the divisions that we are looking at in this book. You might perhaps feel the same on reading Jesus' terrible oracle about Jerusalem, the city that on the whole its inhabitants tended to assume had the divine favour. See 21:20-24, and particularly its chilling conclusion: 'Jerusalem will be trodden by the Gentiles, until the times of the Gentiles are fulfilled'. This is not an easy Gospel.

Some thoroughly uncomfortable stories

Luke is the best of the four evangelists at telling memorable stories, a great painter with words; but his gentle tone tends to blind us to the fact that some of the stories have very uncomfortable implications. Consider, for example, chapter 16, where there are two stories to make us uneasy. The first is the story of the Steward (16:1-8), who is given the sack (on hearsay evidence and with no chance to defend himself, see 1, 2), and decides to make something of his unhappy situation by giving his master's creditors a bit extra on the side. This story comes right after the three challenging stories that we looked at earlier, the Lost Sheep, the Lost Coin, and the Lost Son of chapter 15; and it ends in this remarkable way: 'The Lord praised the steward of iniquity because he had acted intelligently; because the children of this age are more intelligent that the sons of light with regard to their own generation.' It may be that Luke himself was a bit puzzled by the story, because he adds to it a series of statements concerning money (always a divisive phenomenon, of course), which do not notably serve to explain it (see 16:9-13).

This story is followed by the equally uncomfortable parable of Lazarus and the rich man (16:19-31), with its unmistakable condemnation of the wealthy, and the division between where the rich end up (Hades, v.23), and where the poor go ('the bosom of Abraham', even if they do not have the money to get buried; see v.22). They have to listen to Moses and the prophets (v.31).

And there are other stories: the first one is what we might in our day call 'the Grateful Immigrant' (17:11-19), the unforgettable story of the Ten Lepers. They all address him appropriately enough as 'Jesus, Master', and ask him for 'mercy'; he simply tells them, 'Off you go – show yourselves to the priests,' and they are cured on the way! What happens next, though, is pertinent to our quest for divisions and how to handle them. For the only one to express gratitude is the 'grateful immigrant', a Samaritan (and we have already seen one story where such a foreigner was the hero), who 'on seeing that he had been healed, turned back with a loud cry, glorifying God. And he fell on his face at his feet, giving him thanks – and he was a Samaritan!' Jesus' comment at the end makes it clear that it was the religious and cultural outsider who got it right: 'Rise up and go on your journey; your faith has saved you.' We might reflect on how this story deals with the divisions in our world.

A second such story is the one I call 'the Judge's Black Eye' (18:1-7), where a judge 'who has no fear of God nor respect for human beings', and is therefore likely to be a source of division (injustice always works that way), eventually gives in to the impetration of a widow (like Samaritans, a favoured character in Luke), reflecting that 'even though I have no fear of God or respect for human beings, because this widow is giving me hassle, I am going to give her the verdict, otherwise she'll come and give me a black eye!' This is what the text means, but translators are often a bit coy about that, for some reason.

Then there are the 'two ways of praying' (18:9-14), where we watch in astonishment as Jesus tells the story of the Pharisee and the Tax Collector; both of these rather stock characters are found praying in the Temple. We expected one, but not the other; and we notice the divisions between them. The Pharisee tells the truth: he really is religiously observant, congratulating God on having 'me as your servant', greatly superior to the rest of humanity (especially 'this tax collector'), because of his fasting twice a week and paying tithes. The tax collector, on the other hand, a thoroughly bad person, a traitor and a dealer in unclean goods, inclined to exploit his power against his compatriots, simply prays, paying attention only to God, striking his breast in repentance as he does so: 'God, have mercy on me, the sinner.' Then comes the electrifying verdict: 'This one went down home justified, not the other one'! We can hardly believe such a thing, but our divisions would be a great deal less serious if we could only reflect on that parable.

Of a piece with this is the story that we might call 'the Generosity of a Widow' (21:1-4). Once again there is a contrast between rich and poor; and we know that in our society this is an appalling source of division. Here you have, on the one hand, all the wealthy putting their huge sums into the collecting boxes at the Temple, and by contrast, the poor widow who puts in a couple of tiny coins. We may imagine the complacent sneer of the wealthy at this trivial contribution. But then listen to Jesus' comment:

> 'Truly I'm telling you that this widow, destitute as she is, threw in more than all of them. For all of them threw in what came from their surplus, into the gifts; but she put in what came from her deficit; she threw her entire life [using the same phrase as the evangelist had used for the prodigal father in chapter 15] that she had.'

Learning to see as Jesus sees will certainly help us cope with divisions.

Remarkably, for such a non-violent Gospel, the disciples get into a fight at the long-awaited Passover meal (22:24-30). And what is it about? What, alas, Christians have too often fought about ever since: 'Which of us seems to be the most important?' They have to be taught Jesus' way ('eyes on Jesus', once again, you see): 'I am with you as one who serves.' This is a hint, of course, that John's account of the Last Supper elevates into the wonderfully unifying story of the washing of the disciples' feet.

Lastly in this section we have an unedifying example of divisions united: Herod and Pilate (23:12). You will remember how this happens; in the course of his interrogation of Jesus, Pilate discovers that Jesus is a Galilean, and uses this as an excuse to get rid of him to Herod, who is luckily in Jerusalem for the Passover festival. Herod makes nothing of him, does not get to see any of the conjuring tricks that he was hoping for, and in frustration sends him back to Pilate. Then we get Luke's comment on the episode: 'Herod and Pilate became friends with each other on that day; for previously they had been at enmity with each other.' You can interpret that how you will, of course; you might argue that Jesus even here heals divisions, or you might want to say that the forces of injustice cling to each other in the face of his threat. Either way, this passage has something to say to our quest.

Signs of hope in the face of division

However, Luke's Gospel is not all about divisions; it ends (or we should not bother to read it) with signs of hope. The women of Jerusalem, paradoxically at the moment when Jesus is coming to his terrible end, offer just such a sign (23:27-30), precisely because they stand out against what is going on, and then Jesus unselfishly diverts the tears away from himself and towards them: 'Daughters of Jerusalem, don't weep over me, but over yourselves and over your children.' In this impossibly divided situation, both Jesus and the women who are mourning over him are looking beyond themselves to the Other; and that is the answer to all our divisions.

But did the women get it wrong? Luke tells us, almost at the end of his Gospel, that 'in the deep dawn they came to the tomb, carrying the spices they had bought – and they found the stone rolled away from the tomb' (24:1, 2). Then they are identified (24:10, 11): 'Mary Magdalen, and Joanna and Mary of Jacob and the other women with them; they told these things to the apostles; and these words seemed like babbling to them. And they did not believe them.' This negative verdict is then confirmed by Cleopas and his companion, who are trudging miserably to Emmaus with the one person who could confirm the truth (24:22-4): 'But some women from us amazed us. They came early to the tomb, and when they did not find his body they came saying that they had seen a vision of angels, who said he was alive!' (Here we can almost hear them adding the clause – 'but you know what women are'.) And the women, not for the first or the last time, have it right, and there is hope in the midst of the divisions, for Jesus is risen (which means that all our divisions will not be the end of the story).

Finally in this Gospel, all divisions come to an end (though only for a while, as we saw in the chapter on Acts of the Apostles) with the final appearance of the Risen Jesus, in what I call the story of the alarming ghost (24:36-45). They are not at all heartened (are we?) by the appearance of the Risen One, but 'became fearful and thought that they were looking at a spirit!' So they are still divided, and have to be reproached for it; then they are offered evidence: wounded hands and feet, and when they still do not believe ('out of joy', as Luke remarks with characteristic charity), he asks for a piece of fish, and eats it before their astonished gaze.

So there you have it: there are divisions in the Church, and they are to be expected; the solution is simply, as always in our New Testament texts, to keep our eyes on God and on Jesus, and that should put an end to our divisions. But will we do it?

Conclusion

Luke, then, who is the best storyteller among the evangelists, and unafraid to tell tales that are thoroughly uncomfortable, nevertheless offers us ways of coping with our divisions. He starts with the devout silence of Mary, and stresses the 'importance of the unimportant'; this is helpful because many of our divisions spring from my sense that I am more important than you. Luke also reminds us that religious discourse can be divisive, and that we need to school our speech in the direction of generosity, if we are to do anything about our divisions. He also reminds us that Jesus is himself a divisive figure, one who is doomed to die; Jesus in Luke's Gospel is also a socially uncomfortable character, as we saw in the 'disastrous dinner-parties'. There is perhaps no simple way forward out of our divisions.

CHAPTER 9

Revelation and divisions

We come, then, to the last book of our Bible, the Book of Revelation. And this book has much to teach us, not least that we have a great deal to learn from other Christians, from religious people who are not Christian, and from those who do not believe in God. Revelation is a most extraordinary text; you might describe it as 'songs of unity in the face of persecution', although there is much more to it than that. And there is a great deal here to be said about divisions in the Church.

Seven letters to seven different churches

What kind of a document is Revelation? That is an important question, if we are to see what it has to tell us today about divisions in the Church. The document describes itself in at least three different ways. The very first word (1:1), almost its title, is *apokalypsis*, which means 'uncovering' and gets translated into Latin as *revelatio*, which means 'unveiling'. So it sees itself as a lifting of the veil, to give the reader (or hearer) a glimpse of what is going on.

It also, however, calls itself a *propheteia*, which turns, of course, into the English word 'prophecy'; but we must remember that this does not mean prediction, so much as a statement of what is God's view of the world. The word reappears towards the end, at 22:7, 10, 18, 19, where the repetition suggests that the author wants us to see it as the best way of understanding the scroll; and it comes with 'congratulations' (v.7) to those who 'keep the words of the prophecy of this scroll', and warnings against adding to them (v.18), or taking anything from them (v.19).

The text is also called a 'scroll' or 'book' (1:11; 10:8; 20:12; 22:7, 9, 10, 18, 19), a site for storing the mysterious business of making marks on papyrus so that they can be read out and so revealed. And at the beginning it even looks like a letter, for at 1:4 we hear the typical ancient letter-form: 'John, to the seven churches which are in Asia, grace to you and peace'. So there are several different clues as to what this all might be, and we shall do well not to be too definite about it.

But there is plenty of division; one of the most interesting places to look for this is in chapters 2 and 3, where the seer has seven letters dictated to him, to send to seven churches. Have a look at the map, and if you look at where they are and how they are connected, you will observe that the seven cities, which are linked by excellent Roman roads, are mentioned in the order in which a messenger might visit them. So we are talking here about the real world, one in which there are real divisions, to continue our quest for how the New Testament authors dealt with the problem of inter-Christian discord.

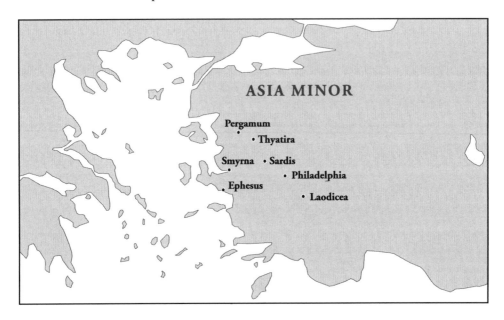

The first letter is to the Christians in Ephesus (2:1-7). This ancient Greek city was colonised by Ionian Greeks way back in the eleventh century BC. If you ever have the chance to visit, you will see that it was absolutely magnificent, the capital of the Roman Province of Asia, with an excellent harbour, now alas silted up, and a theatre that could seat 25,000, where the acoustics are to this day very impressive indeed. The Temple of Artemis there was one of the seven wonders of the ancient world. There was a basilica to the Emperor Augustus, which of course those early Christians could not possibly countenance. And, according to Acts of the Apostles chapter 19, Paul was there; and riots by silversmiths broke out because he was damaging the worship of Artemis, their favourite deity: 'Great is Artemis of the Ephesians,' they cried, angrily (Acts 19:28).

So it is a real city, and there are signs of real divisions: at Revelation 2:2, John congratulates them because 'you cannot put up with evil people', and because 'you tested those who call themselves apostles and are not, and you found them liars'. We have no idea what are the issues that he is speaking of here, but they were evidently real, and the Ephesians knew perfectly well what he was talking about. They are also praised because (v.6) 'you hate the Nicolaitans'. Sadly, we do not know who these characters were, but they are clearly on the wrong side of the divisions, as far as our author is concerned. Not that there is unmixed praise for the Ephesian Christians, because they are told at verse 5 that 'you need to repent'. Once again it is not clear what they have got wrong, but clearly there is trouble there in Ephesus.

The second letter is to Smyrna (2:8-11). This city, now known as Izmir, had an excellent harbour, and lay at the western end of a major road, and had a temple to Dea Roma, 'the goddess Rome', which would have horrified the Christian community. Once again, the author knows what has gone wrong there, and so do his audience, while we can only guess what he means when he speaks (v.9) of 'the blasphemy of those who say they are Jews and are not, but the synagogue of Satan'. Once again we are clearly treading on the edge of serious divisions, but cannot say what they involved. The answer, however, is always the same: eyes on Jesus, 'the first and the last, who became dead and was alive'.

The third letter is to the Christians in Pergamum (2:12-17), one of the loveliest of the Greek cities in the first century, which is in the Mysia region, and had an excellent library and a school of sculpture. The letter contains a reference to 'Satan's throne', which might refer to the Temple of Zeus, or to emperor worship, or possibly to the courts of the imperial government (the governor alone was allowed to exercise capital punishment). There was also a shrine there of Asclepius, the god of medicine, seen by some as a rival to Christ. Here, too, there are divisions, for we read in verse 13 that 'Antipas my witness was killed among you . . . where Satan dwells', and that, according to verse 14, 'some of you hold the teachings of Balaam', and in verse 15 there is a reference once more to the mysterious Nicolaitans, who clearly have to do with divisions of some kind in the infant Church. So we are made aware that such divisions are nothing new.

Next comes the letter to the Christians at Thyatira (2:18-29). I hope that you are still keeping an eye on the map, to see how our messenger's journey is going to these divided cities. If so, you will see that it lies between Pergamum and Sardis, on the Lycus River. Once again, there are complaints which we cannot fully understand, that they are prepared to tolerate 'Jezebel, who says she is a prophetess, and teaches and leads astray my slaves to "fornicate" and to eat food offered to idols' (2:20). Clearly, whatever 'Jezebel' has been doing, and whoever she may be, she is creating divisions of some kind in those parts. Whatever the issue may be, it is clearly quite serious (2:21-5):

> I have given her time to repent; but she is not willing to repent of her fornication. Look – I am throwing her on a bed, and those who commit adultery with her, into a great tribulation, if they do not repent of her deeds. And I am going to kill her children with death; and all the churches shall know that I Am the One who interrogates the reins and the hearts,

and I am going to give each of you in accordance with your deeds. I am telling the rest of you in Thyatira, those who do not hold to this teaching, those who did not know the depths of Satan, as they say: I am not imposing on you any other burden: but hold on to what you have, until I come.

The fifth letter is to the Christians of Sardis (3:1-6). This city was the capital of Lydia; it had been conquered by the Persians in the sixth century BC, then again by Alexander in 334BC, and then became a provincial capital for the Seleucid Empire. It was thoroughly Hellenised, and by this time had become a centre for emperor worship. Once again there is something wrong in this church, and John's correspondents know whom he is talking about: 'you have some people [names, verse 4] who have not defiled their garments', and others will have their names wiped out of the book of life (v.5). This presumably means that at least some people, whom we may imagine complacently purring as this is read out in their church, are not in this unhappy situation.

The sixth letter (3:7-13) is to Philadelphia, which is likewise to be found in Lydia. This lively city had been founded by Attalus II of Pergamum in the second century BC, and had important trade links with other similar cities: Sardis, Pergamum, Laodicea and Hierapolis. It lived mainly off agriculture, the sale of leather, and textiles. Once again there is something that they know about and we do not, which the elder John speaks of as 'synagogue of Satan' (again, verse 9), 'of those who call themselves Jews and are not, but are telling untruths'. The vision tells us that 'I'll make them come and bow down before your feet, and know that I loved you.' Clearly we are eavesdropping here on some kind of division in the early Church, even if we cannot say what it was. Once again, the answer is to keep their eyes on God and on Jesus.

The final community to be addressed is that of the wealthy city of Laodicea (3:14-21). Laodicea is in the relatively wealthy region of Phrygia; it had been founded by Antiochus II, and named after his wife. The important cities of Colossae and Hierapolis lay nearby, in the same river valley. You will observe the often-cited reference to their being 'lukewarm', and this may have been because of the splendid aqueduct that linked Laodicea with the hot springs at nearby Hierapolis, which would inevitably reduce the temperature at which the water reached the city, and made 'lukewarm' a suitable metaphor for the faith of its Christians, who are described (vv.15,16) as 'neither hot nor cold but lukewarm', and told (v.17) that 'you say, "I am rich" and "I have become rich" and "I have no need"'. This is the kind of thing that Christians in any age who find themselves living in a wealthy culture might unconsciously be saying to themselves.

So these letters are not 'private correspondence', but really important for understanding the world into which the Book of Revelation is addressed, and we are not to rush on to the 'serious business' of the text without taking them on board.

Eavesdropping on the heavenly liturgy

After that all-important introduction, chapters 4 to 6 present us with a Church united in liturgy around God and the Lamb. It is not permitted to us to rush past the liturgy, as we are sometimes tempted to do, for liturgy is not 'irrelevant', but gives us the shape of God's response to our broken world, and the response that we are invited to make ourselves. Liturgy can reach the parts, as the old advertisement used to say, that other religious activities cannot reach; and if we understand it correctly, it functions extremely well as a model for coping with division. Everyone, including the elders, and the visionary, are singing (literally) from the same hymn-sheet.

The message of all this is that there is nothing to be afraid of: all is known to God. There is not much here on division, but I suggest that before continuing to read this chapter you spend some time listening to the liturgy of chapters 4 to 6, and noticing how it invites you to keep your eyes on God and on the Lamb. Then you can proceed to chapter 7, and listen to the number of those who are 'sealed'; the reader is invited to have confidence in the face of the tensions of the contemporary world, as we are given the 'number of those who have been sealed' (7:4). The number is 144,000, and the passive, 'are sealed', implies that it is God who is doing it, and we know that 'all shall be well'. At 7:9, after the numbers of all those drawn from Israel, we read of 'a great crowd, which no one could count'. This presumably means that it is greater than 144,000; and this vast throng is heard singing songs of the Lamb's victory. They are identified (7:14) as 'those who come out of the great tribulation who washed their robes in the Lamb's blood'.

What the liturgy tells us

These liturgical visions, however, do not mean that there is no suffering for Christians. For quite soon we are invited to listen to the rejoicing of the enemies of the Church (11:10): 'those who dwell on the earth rejoice over them and celebrate, and will send each other presents', because they have killed God's two prophets. We do not know who these 'two prophets' might be, but clearly there is a division of some kind between them and the menacing outside world; and John's Christian readers are involved in this division.

The division, however, is not the devastating end of the story, and so at 14:1-3 we are witnesses to a wonderful and reassuring picture of musical unity:

> And I saw, and look! – the Lamb standing on Mount Zion, and with him a hundred and forty-four thousand who have his name, and the name of his Father, written on their foreheads. And I heard a voice from heaven like the voice of many waters, and like the voice of a great thunder.
>
> And the voice which I heard was like the voice of harpists playing harp-melodies on their harps.[97] And they are singing a new song before the Throne and before the four living creatures and before the elders. And no one could learn the song except the hundred and forty-four thousand, who were purchased from the Land.

It is not, to be perfectly honest, absolutely clear what is intended by this, but the flavour is that of victory over divisions.

Then they are further defined (14:4, 5):

> These are the ones who were not defiled with women, for they are virgins.
> These are the ones who follow the Lamb wherever he goes.
> These are the ones who were purchased from humanity,
> the first fruits for God and for the Lamb,
> and in their mouth was found no falsehood – they are unblemished.

There is an unmistakable sense of unity here, and it is to be read (or heard) as an encouragement whether to us, ruefully aware of our divisions, or to those first-century readers who had the added excuse for their divisions that they were enduring a horrendous persecution.

What about Babylon?

The persecution is therefore something that must be considered in this context. The persecutor is described as 'the Great Prostitute', sitting on a 'scarlet beast, full of names of blasphemy, with seven heads and ten horns' (17:3). The prostitute turns out to be code for the great city of Rome, whose destruction is foreseen (17:5, 6):

> on her forehead a name has been written, a mystery 'Babylon the Great',
> the mother of prostitutes and of the abominations of the earth.
> And I saw the woman drunk from the blood of the saints,
> And from the blood of the witnesses [martyrs] of Jesus
> And wondered, when I saw her, a great wonder.

---

97. This slightly cumbersome repetition of 'harp' is meant to pick up the sound of the Greek.

We know that this enemy is not going to survive in the vision that God has granted. More than that, we notice that the Beast, or Dragon, parodies the Lamb, so at 12:16 we have already seen that 'the earth helped the woman and the earth opened its mouth and swallowed up the river which the Dragon poured out of its mouth'. These are the waters of death; and we read (13:2) that 'the Dragon gave [the Beast] its power, and its throne, and great authority'. This is clearly a terrible parody of the relationship between God on his Throne, and the slaughtered Lamb which we glimpsed in the heavenly liturgy. Indeed, 'one of the heads [of the Beast] was as it were slaughtered to death', echoing what happened to the Lamb, except that its 'mortal wound was cured' (13:3). This does not happen to the Lamb; there is no magic for the forces of good. Another element of parody is to be found in 13:3, 4: 'the whole earth . . . went a-wandering after the Beast, and they worshipped the Dragon, because it had given its authority to the Beast'. You can see how this is a pale imitation of the relationship between God and the Lamb.

It also offers a clue as to how we are to deal with our divisions. The 'name of the game' is to avoid the power struggle that the Beast and the Dragon and Babylon the Great go in for. Look, for example, at 13:6, 8:

> And the Beast opened its mouth for blasphemy against God,
> To blaspheme his name and his Tent [a term of rich symbolism in Johannine literature],
> Those who pitch their Tent in heaven. . .
> . . . and all those who dwell on earth shall worship him, those whose name
> is not written in the Scroll of the Lamb Slaughtered
> from the Foundation of the World.

Those who are on the Lamb's side are vulnerable, but sing a song of harmony, and are in the end assured of victory; and they are united by a vision of the truth, whereas the Second Beast (13:11-14)

> had two horns like the Lamb, but spoke like the Dragon
> and does all the authority of the First Beast . . .
> and it does great signs,
> to make fire come down from heaven on the earth
> in the sight of human beings,
> and it leads astray the inhabitants of the earth,
> because of the signs that it was given to do before the Beast,
> telling the inhabitants of the earth
> to make a likeness for the Beast (who has a sword-blow – and lived).

We can only guess at some of the details here, but what is clear is that any divisions among the Christians are to be sorted out according to what side they choose in the battle: the power-hungry Beast or the gentle and vulnerable slaughtered Lamb, who is going to win in the end, because he is on God's side. Our author recognises that Christians suffer, and that they will be vindicated.

Glimpses of the final victory

This is how we are to come to the end of this remarkable book, filled with confidence in the victory that comes from being united around the Throne and the Lamb. So our author brings us towards the climax (20:4):

> I saw thrones and they sat upon them, and judgement was given them;
> [and I saw] the souls of those who had been beheaded
> because of the witness of Jesus and because of the word of God
> and those who had not worshipped the Beast or its likeness
> and did not accept the mark on their forehead and hands,
> and who lived and ruled with Christ.

Then at last we are granted, as the music comes to its glorious conclusion, the final vision of an end to all divisions, creation utterly restored, as in the beginning of the Bible, so at its end (21:1-5):

> And I saw a new heaven and a new earth,
> for the first heaven and the first earth had gone away – and sea was no more.
> And the Holy City, New Jerusalem,
> I saw coming down out of Heaven from God,
> prepared like a bride adorned for her husband.
> And I heard a great voice from the Throne, which said:
> 'Look – God's tent with human beings,
> and he shall pitch his tent with them,
> and they shall be his peoples, and he God with them, shall be their God.
> And he shall wipe away every tear from their eye
> And Death shall be no more,
> Nor grief, nor wailing, nor distress shall be any more,
> For the former things have gone.'

It is a wonderful picture, and suddenly all divisions have disappeared, simply because they are united in gazing on this new vision that comes from God.

Conclusion

So we come to the end, and it is a majestic conclusion (22:14-17):

> Congratulations to those who wash their robes,
> in order that their authority may be over the Tree of Life
> and they may enter the City by the gates.
> Out go the dogs and the drug-dealers and the fornicators and murderers
> and idolators and everyone who is a lover and a doer of falsehood.
> I, Jesus, sent my messenger to give witness to you people
> in regard to the churches.
> I am the Root and Stock of David, the Bright Morning Star
> And the Spirit and the Bride say, 'Come.'
> And the one who hears says, 'Come.'
> And let the one who thirsts come.
> The one who wishes, let them take the water of life for free.

So there you have it, a stunning vision, and not the terrifying visions that the Book of Revelation is often thought to offer, but the picture of undying unity, shorn of divisions, of those who keep their eyes on God and on the Lamb. That is the way ahead for us all.

CHAPTER 10

Divisions in the Catholic Epistles

So we come to our last set of New Testament texts, and the alert reader will not be surprised to find once more what has been a theme in this book, that divisions are always to be expected (but not complacently accepted) in the Church; they tell us something important about how the Spirit might be leading, but we have also to work to overcome them. It is important that we should beware rigidity, and avoid our tendency to insist angrily that 'I know what the Church should be like'. It may be that the Spirit has in mind a quite different vision of the Church from that in which we have grown up, and which we hold dear. It is certain that our task, when faced with divisions, as we have seen throughout this book, is the threefold one of keeping our eyes on God, of imitating Jesus, and of listening for the Holy Spirit. It will not be possible in this chapter to say everything that can usefully be said about what we call the 'Catholic Epistles' (James, 1 and 2 Peter, 1–3 John (which we considered in an earlier chapter), and the Letter of Jude), but we shall be looking out for that pattern.

The reason why they are called 'Catholic' is not absolutely clear – possibly because they were thought to be of 'general' interest (that is one meaning of the word 'catholic') – and I have cheated a bit by including first in this chapter the Letter to the Hebrews, which is not technically one of them. In effect, I mean by 'Catholic Epistles' nothing more than 'everything in the New Testament that we have not mentioned so far'.

The Letter to the Hebrews

Eyes on Jesus

This extraordinary letter, whose theology might loosely be summed up in the phrase 'Jesus is the Real Thing', certainly keeps us gazing at Jesus all the way through. Its deeply theological appeal is always backed up by appeal to Scripture, and the author is absolutely clear that their belief should make a difference to the way the readers of his letter behave.

Now I have already twice called this document a 'letter', and that is how it is often described; indeed, towards the end, at 13:23-5, it behaves like a Pauline letter, with a mention of 'our brother Timothy', and the greetings to the 'leaders', and the salutations offered by 'those from Italy', and the concluding salutation of 'grace be with all of you'. But if you look at how it begins, that is not at all the feeling that it gives; it sounds from the outset more like a theological treatise, and that is how it continues, although it also has a good deal to say about how we should behave. For our purposes in this book we do not need to decide this question, but keep it in your mind as you read.

Some general problems in the community

The first thing to say is that whoever it was to whom Hebrews is addressed, they have had difficulties in the community. So at 10:25 they are warned that they should not 'give up the assembly, as is some people's custom, and all the more as you see the day approaching'.

Failure to attend church, however, is not the only problem here. For at 13:1-3 the author stresses the importance of the ideas conveyed by two Greek words, *philadelphia* and *philoxenia*; the first of these means 'love of the brothers and sisters', and the second is 'love of foreigners' [or might we say 'immigrants'?]. This comes with the supporting argument that some people have 'given hospitality to angels' (which is presumably meant to remind us of the splendid story of Abraham giving hospitality to God (Genesis 18:2; 19:1). Then they are instructed to remember the imprisoned, 'as though you were in with them, and those who are badly treated, as though you are in the body'. This is presumably a hint of ways in which the community has failed in the recent past, and the kind of area in which we might look for their divisions.

Then there is another useful admonition, at 13:7: 'Remember your leaders who spoke the Word of God to you: have a good look at the result of their life, and imitate their faith.' It is always tempting to blame leaders for things going wrong, and something of the sort may have been happening in this community.

Some particular problems: 'apostasy'

In particular, the group has known temptations to apostasy. They are warned (2:1, 2) to pay attention to the things that they have heard, 'lest we drift away', and to focus (2:3, 4) on 'what was spoken through the Lord' and on 'God who testifies at the same time with signs and portents and different kinds of miracles and different kinds of gifts of the Holy Spirit in accordance with his will'. Once again, you see, even though we cannot quite say what the divisions are, the answer to them lies in paying attention to 'Father, Son and Holy Spirit'.

The same threat of 'apostasy' is considered when they are warned (3:12-14):

Watch out, brothers and sisters: there is not to be, ever, an evil heart among you, of unbelief, to apostatise from the living God. Instead, you must comfort one another, day after day, until the one [day] comes that is called 'Today', so that none of you gets 'hardened' by the seduction of sin. You see, we have become sharers in Christ . . .

Once more there is an emphasis on the importance of proper authority, as they are urged (4:11) that no one 'should fall by an example of disobedience'. Or, similarly, we are to show obedience (and we have to admit that this is not a fashionable virtue in our day, but it may be time for a revival) to the faith, as we read at 4:14: 'Since we have a High Priest who has gone through the heavens, Jesus the Son of God, let us hold on to our confession.' The theme reappears at 6:6, with a warning against 'falling aside . . . crucifying the Son of God for themselves and making an example'.

The idea of apostasy reappears at 10:26, under the notion of 'voluntary sinning on our part after we have received knowledge of the Truth, and there is no longer any sacrifice for sins'. Three verses later there are said to be (10:29) serious sanctions for 'trampling down the Son of God, regarding the blood of the covenant as profane . . . and insulting the Spirit of grace'. Then at 10:39 they are warned not to belong to 'those who have timidity, which leads to destruction, but to those who have faith for acquiring life'. All of these hint at divisions in that community, the precise shape of which we cannot confidently reconstruct, but of whose existence there can be no possible doubt. The members of that community will have known what the author was talking about.

A strategy for coping

In the face of these divisions, however, there is a strategy for coping, in the shape of a common confession about Jesus (something that has been evident to us throughout this book). So he is declared to be the 'originator of our salvation' (2:10) or the 'missionary and High Priest of our confession' (3:1), or (4:14) the 'great High Priest who has gone through the heavens', which is a reason for 'holding on to the confession', so that we are to 'hold on to the confession unswervingly – because the One who gave the promise is reliable' (10:23). The point here is that divisions are to be dealt with by holding on to what we have, and keeping our eyes fixed on God and on Jesus.

Importantly, however, we have to cope with our divisions by recognising our humanity as shared with Jesus: 'the one who makes [us] holy, and [we] who are being made holy come from the same stock . . . the children have shared the flesh and blood', which makes it possible to 'cancel out the Devil' (2:11-14). It is essential (4:14, 15) to recognise our likeness to Jesus, as well as our tendency to give in to sin. And so (5:11, 12) we have to admit that we fall short of where we should be, and our need, not for solid food, but, like babies, for 'milk'.

The way ahead

And there is for this community a way ahead, which is sketched out at 6:18-20:

> Through two unchangeable things, in which it is impossible for God to be deceived ... we have the hope that lies before us as a safe and secure anchor for our life, one that goes into the inner sanctuary where Jesus entered on our behalf as forerunner, becoming a priest in accordance with the order of Melchisedek for ever.

Once again, the answer to our divisions is to cling firmly to God and to Jesus, recognising (10:19-23) what Jesus has achieved for us, and putting our trust firmly in him. Or (12:2, 3) we are to follow Jesus' example and leadership, without giving up. We are to cope with our divisions by acknowledging (12:14) the importance of peace and 'sanctification'. As always in the early Church, there are in this document practical instructions on how to stay together (13:4):

> Marriage is to be honoured by everybody, and the marriage-bed undefiled

which may suggest that there were practical as well as theological reasons for divisions in the community. Our life with Jesus is different (13:13, 14):

> therefore let us go out to him, outside the camp, bearing his reproach. For we do not have here an abiding city. No – we are looking for the city that is to come.

We must, therefore, expect to follow Jesus in his suffering, and above all avoid getting too rigid, thinking that we already have it all.

It seems that coping with our divisions may not be as difficult as we might have supposed.

The Letter of James

The remainder of the 'Catholic Epistles' we can deal with more swiftly. Next in your New Testament you will find the Letter of James. We do not know who the author is, though some scholars regard it as possible that he is 'James the brother of the Lord'. He describes himself as 'slave of God and of the Lord Jesus Christ' and addresses himself to 'the 12 tribes which are in the Diaspora'; that, and the high quality of his Greek, suggests that he is writing to those Jews, in the main Greek-speaking, who lived outside of the Holy Land. As with Hebrews, so in respect of this document, there is some question about what kind of thing it is. We call it a 'letter', mainly because it is not a gospel, but it does not really bear the marks of a letter. Some scholars classify it as a 'synagogue homily', but it may be best to admit that we do not quite know what kind of thing it is.

At all events, the author is well aware of divisions in the Church. For one thing, he attests the existence of social tensions in the group that he is addressing. Consider the sharp satire of this passage (2:1-7):

> My brothers and sisters, you are not to make the faith of our Lord Jesus Christ of glory a matter of snobbery. Here is an example: someone comes into your synagogue, a man with gold rings and a resplendent suit; and then someone with no money at all comes in, wearing filthy clothes. Then you look at the person wearing the resplendent suit, and you say, 'You, please, have a nice seat here.' And to the person with no money you say, 'You – stand there', or 'Sit underneath my kneeler' – aren't you in that case making distinctions among yourselves, and turning into bad-minded critics?

> Listen, my beloved brothers and sisters: is it not the case that God chose those who have no money in the world [to be] rich in faith, and heirs of the Kingdom which he promised to those who love him? But you dishonoured the person who had nothing. Is it not the case that the wealthy lord it over you? Is it not they who drag you to the courts? Is it not they who insult that good name that was called down upon you?

Or consider the bleak humour of this passage (2:15,16):

> If a brother or sister has no clothing and lacks anything to eat, and one of you says to them, 'Go in peace; get yourself warm and well-fed', but you fail to give them their bodily needs, what's the use of that?

We are surely not wrong in discerning here the kinds of tension that down the course of history have threatened the unity of the Church. And then there are doctrinal issues. Many people find in the following passage signs of tension with followers of Paul, who, especially in Galatians and Romans, emphasised the importance of 'faith' over against 'works' (2:18-26):

> But someone will no doubt say, 'You may have "faith", and I have "works"': show me your 'faith apart from works', then I'll show you my 'faith that comes out of works'. You believe that God is One: well done – but even the demons believe [this]. And they shudder.

> You empty-headed fool! Do you want evidence that faith apart from works fails to work? Wasn't our ancestor Abraham justified as a result of works when he offered his son Isaac on the altar? You see that faith works along with its 'works'; and faith is made complete [precisely]

from 'works', and the Scripture text is fulfilled, the one that says 'Abraham had faith in God, and it was reckoned to him for justification' – and he was called 'friend of God'. Do you see that a person is justified as a result of 'works', and not just as a result of 'faith'? Similarly, the prostitute Rahab: was she not justified as a result of her 'works', when she gave hospitality to the messengers, and sent them by a different route? You see, just as the body is dead without the spirit, so faith is dead without 'works'.

Whether this is an attack on Paul himself or on his followers, or whether there is some other issue here, there is no mistaking the potential for division. And what is the answer? You pay careful attention to Scripture – keep your eyes on God.

Another piece of evidence in the search for divisions comes in James' reflection on the dangers of the tongue. He insists on the need for chastity in what we say (3:1, 2):

Not many of you ought to become teachers, brothers and sisters; be aware that we [who are teachers] will receive a worse punishment. For we all stumble in many ways. If a person does not stumble in what they say, that is a perfect grown-up, one who is able to bridle the whole body.

Then the author sees the possibility of the idea of a 'bridle' or 'bit', something that was a regular part of their experience in that world, and continues, before going on to another metaphor, that of fire (3:3-12):

Given that we put bridles into horses' mouths, so that they obey us, and we direct their entire bodies, and (look!) those huge ships, which are driven by harsh winds, are directed by the tiniest rudder, wherever the desire of the helmsman leads him. In just the same way the tongue, a tiny organ, does great boasting.

Or look: a tiny fire can burn up an immense wood. And the tongue is a fire. It is a world of iniquity put among our organs which defiles the entire body, and sets fire to the course of existence, inflamed by Gehenna. For all of nature, wild animals and birds, creepy-crawlies and sea-creatures, are being tamed and have been tamed by human beings. But as for the tongue, no human being is ever able to tame it: it is an unstable evil, full of lethal poison. With the tongue we can bless our Lord and Father; and with it we are able to curse fellow human beings who have come to be in the image of God. From one and the same mouth comes blessing and cursing. It should not be like this, brothers and sisters. Surely a spring does not pour out from one and the same opening both sweet and bitter water? Brothers and sisters, can a fig tree produce olives or a vine produce figs? Nor can a salt spring produce sweet water.

The author is clearly well acquainted with the divisions that can be created by the tongue, as he reveals in the following passage[98] (4:1-12):

> Where do the wars among you, and where do the battles come from? Is it not from this, from the pleasures that are fighting in your limbs: you desire, but do not possess, you kill and are jealous; you do not possess because you do not ask? You ask and you do not receive, because you are asking in the wrong way, for something to spend on your pleasures ... *So be subordinated to God, resist the devil, and he will flee from you. Draw near to God, and God will draw near to you* ... Be humbled before the Lord, and he will raise you up. Don't speak against one another, brothers and sisters. The one who speaks against their brother or sister or condemns them speaks against the Law and condemns it; but if you condemn the Law, you are not doing the Law but condemning it. There is one Law-Giver and Judge, the One who can save and destroy. But who are you who condemn your neighbour?

The one who wrote these words is well aware that there are tensions in the community; and notice the remedy for which he reaches, the words in verses 7 and 8, printed in *italic*: they are to focus on God. This remedy is the one we should aspire to today.

One remaining source of divisions in the church that James is addressing is the socio-economic, which the author describes as follows (5:1-6):

> Come now, you rich: weep and mourn over the humiliations that are coming upon you. Your wealth has rotted and your clothes have been devoured by moths. Your gold and silver has rusted; and their rust is going to be evidence against you and will devour your flesh like fire. You stored up treasure for the last days. Look! The unpaid wages of the workers who mowed your lawns are crying out against you; and the cries of the harvesters have reached the ears of the Lord of Hosts. You lived for pleasure on earth and indulged yourselves grossly; you fed your hearts on the day of slaughter. You condemned the just one and put him to death, he does not resist you.

Our author is quite outspoken about what he sees as the cause of divisions in the Church: some of the faithful have far too much money and their hearts are in the wrong place. Could these words be justly addressed to us today?

---

98. It has to be said that the events of the Reformation were immensely complicated by what people said and thought about each other, and we need to learn from this today.

1 Peter

The next book in our New Testament likewise has some thoughts on what to do about divisions. In places, you might think of it as 'How to live with other people', and the answer, as always throughout this book, is that we are to focus on the Lord. One good example of this is the meditation on different meanings of the word *stone* (rather clumsily using the device of italics to signal how it works out), which you will find in the second chapter (1-8):

Put aside all evil and all trickery and fakery and jealousy and defamation; like newborn cubs you should long for milk without trickery, that by means of it you may grow into salvation, once you have experienced by tasting that the Lord is kind [the reader needs to know that this could also sound like 'the Lord is Christ'].

You are to come to him, a living *stone*, which has been rejected by human beings, but for God a chosen and precious one.

And you yourselves, like living *stones*, are being built up, as a spiritual house into a holy priesthood, to offer acceptable spiritual sacrifices to God through Jesus Christ, because as it says in Scripture:

Look! I am placing a *stone* in Sion,
a corner-*stone*, chosen and precious; the one who believes in him
will not be put to shame.
The preciousness is for you who believe,
but to those who do not believe,
a *stone* which the builders rejected,
this is the [*stone*] that has become head-of-the-corner and
a *stone* of stumbling, and a *rock* of *tripping-over-a-pebble* [the Greek here
is *skandalon*, which means a *stone* on which you stub your toe or trip up].

So this meditation on the stone which is Christ, on whom we are all built up, offers a way of coping with our divisions, one that can still speak to us today.

Another source of division in the history of Christianity is the question of how to deal with non-Christian institutions. Here the answer is to present a tolerable exterior (2:11, 12):

Beloved, I am begging you as people who are immigrants and do not belong, steer clear of fleshly desires, which are fighting against your soul.
Always have good conduct among the Gentiles,
so that when people slander you as being evil-doers, they can observe on the basis of your good deeds, and glorify God on the Day of Visitation.

Then there is the question of how to deal with political authorities, and the answer is that Christians are to venerate them (2:13-17):

> Be subordinated to every human creation on account of the Lord,
> whether the emperor since he is in authority,
> or procurators, since they are sent to wreak vengeance on evil-doers
> and give credit to those who do good . . .
> Do it in freedom, not like people who use freedom as a way of concealing evil;
> do it as God's slaves.
> Honour everybody; love the brothers and sisters;
> fear God – honour the emperor.

Above all, for our author, the way to deal with divisions is to have Christ as your model (2:21-5):

> This is what you were called for, because Christ suffered on your behalf,
> leaving an example for you, that you might follow in his footsteps,
> 'who did not do sin;
> nor was guile found in his mouth'.

> When he was reviled, he did not revile in return; when he suffered he did not indulge in threats, but handed himself over to the One who judges justly. He himself carried our sins in his body on the tree, in order that we might come to life, having nothing to do with sins; by his wound you were healed.
> For you people were wandering like sheep; but now you have turned back to the Shepherd and overseer of your souls.

(Here the author is quoting Isaiah 53; and compare 3:13-18 for the way Christ offers a model for dealing with divisions.)

Above all they are to avoid divisions (3:8, 9):

> To end, all of you should be of one mind and one feeling, loving the brothers and sisters, compassionate and of a humble disposition. Don't pay back evil for evil, or a curse for a curse. On the contrary, you are to give a blessing, because this is what you have been called for, in order to inherit a blessing.

Finally, they are given instructions on how to look after the group (5:1-4):

> I am begging you elders (I am an elder along with you, and a witness of the sufferings of Christ), and also a sharer in the glory that is about to be revealed. You are to shepherd the flock of God that is among you, not under

compulsion, but voluntarily in accordance with God, not for shady profit, but willingly. You are not to 'lord it' over your allotted portions. Instead you must become models for the flock. And when the Chief Shepherd appears, you will win the imperishable reward of the 'gold medal'.

This is a piece of advice that we shall do well to remember today as we cope with our divisions.

2 Peter

There is not quite so much on divisions in 2 Peter, but the author is well aware of dangers in the community, especially those of false teachers and false prophets (2:1, 2):

There arose false witnesses among the people, as indeed there are going to be false teachers among you. They are going to bring in secretly destructive factions [the word means 'choices' and turns into the English word 'heresies'], and deny the Lord who purchased them, bringing a rapid destruction upon themselves. And many people are going to follow their licentiousness, and through them the way of truth is going to be reviled.

The author quite clearly realises that false teachers represent a threat to unity; they are described as 'bold and arrogant . . . they lead unstable people astray, hearts disciplined in greed' (2:10, 14). The answer, however, to all the divisions that they cause is to 'escape the defilements of the world 'by the recognition of our Lord and Saviour Jesus Christ' (2:20); this is by now a familiar enough refrain for us.

Jude

Lastly (for we looked at the three Johannine letters in a previous chapter), there is the Letter of Jude; and this author is likewise aware of the divisions caused by false prophets, who are 'denying our only Master and Lord Jesus Christ' (v.4). He knows, too, of the divisions caused by scoffers, and says of them (vv.19-22):

these are the dividers, unspiritual people, who do not have the Spirit: as for you, beloved, build yourselves up in your most holy faith, pray in the Holy Spirit, keep yourselves in the Love of God, welcome the mercy of our Lord Jesus Christ for eternal life. Have mercy on those who wobble.

So what is the solution? What it has been throughout the entire New Testament – namely, that the answer is to be found in paying attention to God and to Jesus Christ (vv.24, 25):

To the one who can guard you without stumbling, and put you before his glory, blameless in joy, to the Only God our Saviour, through Jesus Christ our Lord, glory, majesty, power and authority before all the ages and now and for ever and ever, Amen.

That is not a bad note on which to end our explorations of the way they dealt with divisions in the New Testament.

Conclusion

Once again, then, we see the same pattern in the 'Catholic Epistles'. Contrary to what we sometimes suppose, there is nothing new about divisions in the Church, and we have seen that each of the authors in this part of the Bible has remedies to offer. We have to beware, whoever we are, of thinking that we know precisely what the Church should look like. All the way through, the answer to our problems of division is (you will be tired of hearing this by now) 'eyes on Jesus'. All communities, including religious communities, experience tension, and that is not the end of the world. The question is what we do about them, even when they come from serious causes such as apostasy. The way ahead remains simple: cling to the Living God; look after the poor.

CHAPTER 11

Is Mary an obstacle to ecumenical progress?

Introduction

Finally, in this book on the divisions that beset Christianity, it seems good to look at the question of Mary, which at first sight seems enormously divisive. In this last chapter I should like to suggest a way ahead out of the divisions, one that (as we have been saying all the way through this book) involves keeping our gaze firmly upon God and upon Jesus.

Sometimes Catholics find ourselves nervously aware that our Protestant brothers and sisters feel that we have invented all sorts of traditions about Mary the Mother of God which are not to be found in Scripture, and that therefore our beliefs about 'Our Lady', as we tend to call her, are late impositions. This is particularly the case with the two teachings about Mary that were only defined in the last century and a half – that Mary was 'immaculately conceived' (a notion that even some Catholics confuse with the 'Virgin Birth') and that she was 'assumed', body and soul, into heaven on her death.

It may be important to make it clear what we are trying to do in this chapter: I am not here trying to convince you, if you do not already believe in what Catholics say about Mary. The aim is rather to let you know what it feels like to be a Catholic in this respect; and you may also be reassured to know that Catholic views of Our Lady are rather more restrained than is supposed by some Christians of the Reformed Tradition (and indeed by some Catholics). The basic argument is that anything that we say about Mary points a) to the truth about Jesus, and then b) to the truth about humanity. Catholic teaching about Mary is never about Mary herself.

Scripture alone?

One important point that we should make is that it has never really been the case in the Church that our beliefs come exclusively from Scripture; indeed, it is rather the other way round, since Scripture comes from the Church. And consider the doctrines of the Trinity and of the *homoousion* (describing Jesus' relationship to the Father), which are held by Christians of all shades. Neither of them is precisely taught in the New Testament; instead they emerge from the life and the worship of the Church, as it tries to live out the gospel message and grapple with its implications. So there is not a great deal about Mary in the New Testament, but in subsequent centuries we have an immense range of patristic and later material, as highly trained theological minds, committed to gospel truth, meditated on the Old Testament, and tried to examine what the Gospels say of Mary, and how it all hangs together.

One developing insight (you will find it as early as Irenaeus in the second century) is that if Mary was to be the Mother of God, then it required a level of personal holiness on her part; this insight was sometimes expressed in terms of Mary's obedience restoring the disobedience of Eve. And the idea that she remained perpetually a virgin is encountered in the Protevangelium of James, as early as the second century; once again, this document, which never made it into the canonical collection, is trying to explicate the mystery of Jesus in its contemporary setting. The question is always: how can Jesus speak today, and how can we speak of Jesus? Eyes, you see, on Jesus, and on God.

Fighting for Jesus' humanity

The real battle is for the humanity of Jesus; and there is a danger that if you do not get Mary right, then you will get the mystery of Jesus wrong. Christian iconography that insists on painting Mary as pregnant, or representing her parents, is dealing with precisely that problem. Jaroslav Pelikan puts it very strongly indeed: 'The most important intellectual struggle of the first five centuries of Christian history – indeed the most important intellectual struggle in all Christian history – took place in response to the question of whether the divine in Jesus was identical with God the Father.'[99] With regard to Mary, these Christian thinkers knew that they had somehow to combine the assertion that Jesus' humanity was real with the denial that Mary was any kind of a goddess. We need to recognise, however, that Catholic belief about Mary was not just a production of 'experts', such as bishops and theologians. In some ways it was ordinary Christians and artists who led the agenda, not the 'institutional Church'. For ordinary Christians wanted to give liturgical expression to the part Mary had played in the history of salvation; and many artists attempted to picture Luke's account of the Annunciation, a scene that graphically brings together the divine and the human which orthodox Christianity combines in its understanding of Jesus. Also in the background there is the deeper question of how you cope with the tension between necessity and free will, between the divine sovereignty and human freedom.

---

99. Jaroslav Pelikan, *Mary through the Ages* (Yale University Press, 1998), p.48.

Theotokos

We cannot in one short chapter say everything that has to be said, but let me begin with the title of 'Theotokos'. The word can be translated, clumsily, as 'the one who gives birth to the one who is God'. The point is that Mary is the Mother of God *incarnate*; obviously God, as such, has no beginning, and therefore no mother.

To call Mary 'Theotokos' is simply a way of preserving the mystery that Jesus cannot be satisfactorily spoken of unless we grasp him as both divine and human (a mind-boggling operation that Christians only undertake because we cannot speak of him in any other way), given that God is ontologically separate from all creation, and yet all humans are creatures.

It was in AD431, at the council of Ephesus, that the Church defined Mary as Theotokos, against the wishes of Nestorius, who wanted to use the term 'Christotokos',[100] to preserve Jesus' full humanity. Cyril, by contrast, wanted to prevent Jesus from being divided into bits.[101] You can see both points of view, of course; but for us, and whichever side you take in that particular debate, we have to grasp that it is all about Jesus, not about Mary. Indeed, it turns out that as Catholics we have a certain flexibility in the matter. This is clear from the common declaration signed by Pope John Paul II and the Assyrian patriarch, Mar Dinkha IV, in 1994 agreeing a common formula, whereby the Assyrian church prays to Mary as 'the Mother of Christ our God and Saviour', while the Catholic Church addresses her as 'the Mother of God and Mother of Christ', and both parties recognise the legitimacy and rightness of these expressions of the same faith.[102] The point is that in endeavouring to talk accurately about Jesus we are on the verge of the impossible.

The great Catholic danger, as an example of this near-impossibility, is that we might lapse into what the reformers regarded as 'Mariolatry'. The Greek word *latreia* is reserved for God alone; to express appropriate reverence for the saints there was the Greek word *douleia*; and for devotion to Mary, the correct term was *hyperdoulia*, which was intended (not always successfully) to prevent devotees from worshipping Mary as a goddess. We might express it like this: being the Mother of God transfigured Mary's human nature. And there was a soteriological dimension to this also, in that Mary foreshadowed God's plan for the restoration of all humanity – that is, that we might be brought back to God's image and likeness. In this context, Mary is no use to us unless she is also a creature, and her dual role of Virgin and Mother performed an important function in Christian thinking about Jesus and about humanity, well expressed

---

100. 'Mother of Christ' rather than 'Mother of God'.
101. Cyril to Nestorius, Letter 3. http://www.voskrese.info/spl/cyr3.html
102. PCPCU, *Information Service* 88 (1995/1), p. 2, cited by Hurley, p. 34.

by Pelikan: 'as the portrait of Mary as the Virgin combatted the perceived excesses of sexuality in Late Antiquity, so the portrait of Mary as the Mother likewise combatted the perceived excesses of asceticism'.[103]

A reformer's view of Mary

The issue remains alive, and in every generation Christian thinkers have continued to explore the mystery, and showed the hold that Mary continues to exercise on the imagination of believers. Do you happen to know who wrote the following words?

> There can be no doubt that the Virgin Mary is in heaven. How it happened we do not know. And since the Holy Spirit has told us nothing about it, we can make of it no article of faith . . . It is enough to know that she lives in Christ.[104]

> [She is the] highest woman and the noblest gem in Christianity after Christ . . . She is nobility, wisdom, and holiness personified. We can never honor her enough. Still honor and praise must be given to her in such a way as to injure neither Christ nor the Scriptures.[105]

> One should honor Mary as she herself wished and as she expressed it in the Magnificat. She praised God for his deeds. How then can we praise her? The true honor of Mary is the honor of God, the praise of God's grace . . . Mary is nothing for the sake of herself, but for the sake of Christ . . . Mary does not wish that we come to her, but through her to God.[106]

> Mary is the Mother of Jesus and the Mother of all of us even though it was Christ alone who reposed on her knees . . . If he is ours, we ought to be in his situation; there where he is, we ought also to be and all that he has ought to be ours, and his mother is also our mother.[107]

> It is a sweet and pious belief that the infusion of Mary's soul was effected without original sin; so that in the very infusion of her soul she was also purified from original sin and adorned with God's gifts, receiving a pure soul infused by God; thus from the first moment she began to live she was free from all sin.[108]

---

103. Pelikan, *Mary through the Ages*, p.122.
104. Sermon on the Feast of the Assumption, 15 August 1522, the last time Martin Luther preached on that solemnity.
105. Christmas Sermon, 1531.
106. Explanation of the Magnificat, 1521.
107. Christmas Sermon, 1529.
108. Sermon On the Day of the Conception of the Mother of God, 1527.

She is full of grace, proclaimed to be entirely without sin – something exceedingly great. For God's grace fills her with everything good and makes her devoid of all evil.[109]

Men have crowded all her glory into a single phrase: The Mother of God. No one can say anything greater of her, though he had as many tongues as there are leaves on the trees.[110]

All of these very charming thoughts, so very Catholic in tone, come, of course, from the pen of Martin Luther, though it would not be accurate to claim that he held all these beliefs at every stage of his life. We have to take seriously the real anxieties of the reformers. Some of the more extreme versions of Marian devotion seemed to them as though Catholics were introducing a goddess, a rival to Jesus and a rival to the God to whom Jesus pointed. They are right to warn us against that tendency, for it is pagan, and we Catholics have to admit that at our worst we are capable of sliding into that form of polytheism.

The secret, to repeat myself, is to recognise that everything that we say about Mary must be either a way of getting Jesus right, or an important statement about human beings, and preferably both. If it is not achieving either or both of these objectives, then it is not orthodox Catholic teaching.

Personal devotion

As I have already indicated, much of the driving of doctrinal formulations about Mary in orthodox Christianity comes from the instincts of ordinary believers, and that very different form of perception that is the gift of artists. Perhaps it might be best if I share with you my own devotion to the Mother of God. For some 50 years I have been in the habit of going to Lourdes to work with the sick people there, and during all that time I have found Mary to be a helpful presence in that place, pointing me, and the hundreds of thousands of pilgrims who visit each year, to her son. And high up in the Rosary Basilica in Lourdes there is written in mosaic 'Par Marie à Jésus' ('through Mary to Jesus'), indicating orthodox Catholic theology on the question.

When I was a child, we sang a hymn to Mary which included the line 'When wicked men blaspheme thee, I'll love and bless thy name'; I had no idea what form such 'blasphemy' might take, but I was determined not to go down that road. I can remember how pained I was when a good friend who is a Christian in the reformed tradition wrote to me that, 'as far as I am concerned, Mary is a

---

109. Personal ('Little') Prayer Book, 1522.
110. From the Commentary on the Magnificat.

sinner, just like the rest of us', and given my background and love for Mary, that sentence was a real shock.

To try to clarify the processes that underlie our Catholic formulations, it may be best to start by looking at what the New Testament has to say about Our Lady.

Scriptural treatment of Mary

When it comes down to it, there is remarkably little, it has to be said, and that is a fact that we have to take seriously. In addition to what I am going to speak of, under the general heading of the New Testament, for completeness it would be proper also to mention Old Testament texts which have fed the imagination of Christian thinkers trying to come to terms with the mystery.

In what I say here, I should like you to test my general proposition that each of these texts are, if they are to work properly, either all about Jesus, or all about human beings, or both.

Galatians 4:4

We start with Paul, the first Christian author to write, in one of his earliest letters. Here the point is that Jesus shares our condition, 'born of a woman' and slavery, and that he came to rescue us from our plight by fully identifying with our problems 'even though he was Lord of all' (the most likely translation of 4:1). This is all about what God is doing in sending Jesus: our attention is on Jesus and on God and on the mess in which human beings find themselves. The basic argument is in 3:26-8: we become sons or daughters of God by accepting Christ, and in baptism, and so there are no distinctions. Jesus has taken on all our human history ('born of a woman, born under the Law'). The text is about Jesus, and what Jesus has done for us, not about his mother.

Although this text is often used in the Catholic tradition for liturgies connected with Mary, that is not Paul's major interest here. Our task when reading all these texts is to bear in mind their original function, and to ask the questions that Paul (and in the next text, Mark) were asking.

Mark 3:20-35

Next we look at Mark, the first of the Gospels to be written. There is not much here, and what there is does not look all that promising. It comes in chapter 3: here Mark produces one of his favourite 'sandwiches', where he wraps two stories one about the other, and invites us to interpret each one by means of the other. The two stories involve a negative reaction to Jesus, from which Mark's readers are invited to dissociate themselves. The central one (verses 22-34) is the terrible accusation by the 'scribes from Jerusalem' that Jesus 'has Beelzeboul' and that 'he expels demons by means of the Ruler of demons'. That is what you might call the 'meat' of the sandwich, in which Jesus effortlessly refutes their allegations, and warns them against the unforgivable blasphemy, against the Holy Spirit. The 'bread' of the sandwich concerns Jesus' family. In the first part (20, 21), we meet what Mark describes as 'those from him', which probably goes best into English as 'his people'. We should notice what they are doing: it is nothing more than anxiety about the fact that he is not eating. There is nothing wrong with this, of course, and we have to understand that in the Mediterranean culture a failure to eat brings shame on the family. So they are behaving perfectly correctly.

The second part of the 'bread' or outer layer of the story is at 3:31-5. For our purposes, we need to notice that Jesus' mother (who is anonymous here) is very prominent. She frames the episode in verses 31 and 35, and the word 'mother' is also used in 32 and 33: 'your mother' and 'my mother'. In this passage the idea of 'mother' (and other family members) is redefined as 'whoever does the will of God'. Clearly there is no sense that Jesus' mother has made the Beelzeboul accusation against him; and it is not so much that his mother is rejected, as that 'those sitting around him' (3:34) are redefined as part of his family. Now it is true that the 'mother and brothers' are 'standing outside, and sent to him, calling him' (3:31), so it might feel like a rejection of the family. Look at it deeper, however, and you will see that it is really a positive statement about the crowds (who are in any case ambiguous in Mark), rather than a negative one about his mother. It is nevertheless uncomfortably challenging, as Mark so often is.[111] The focus, however, is not on Jesus' mother, but on Jesus himself, and how we are to respond to him.

Matthew's three references (1:16, 18; 2:11)

Matthew does not have a great deal more than Mark about Mary; but what he has is interesting. He starts, as all Bible readers know, with the Genealogy,[112] tracing Jesus' descent from Abraham and David, mainly through the male line, but with four interesting women, namely Tamar, Rahab, Ruth and Mrs Uriah.

Why are these four women mentioned? Certainly a part of the answer is that Matthew intends them to shed light on the truth about Mary. There are various possibilities, the standard explanations being either that they were all Gentiles or that they had unconventional domestic relations. A recent book by

---

111. It is interesting that both Matthew (12:46-50) and Luke (8:19-21) in their parallel passages make the story slightly gentler. So they may have felt uncomfortable with it as it stood.
112. 1:1-17.

E. Anne Clements argues that there is a 'gynocentric counter-narrative which centres on Mary'.[113] Mary does not actually do anything, but is made pregnant by God's Holy Spirit (1:18). We should notice the shock of the announcement of Mary's pregnancy, when she and Joseph were only engaged: this is not the way it is supposed to be. Then all the attention is on Joseph, and the child and his mother are dependent for their safety on Joseph and his dreams (1:20-4; 2:13-15, 19-22). We might notice, however, the impact of the citation of Isaiah 7:14, 'the virgin is pregnant, and will bear a son; and they shall call his name Emmanuel'. They do not, of course, actually give Jesus that name; but at the very end of the Gospel, in 28:20, we hear him say '*I am* with you all the days', and at that point we recognise him as 'Emmanuel', which is only possible because of what Mary has done.

There is one other thing to note, namely the oddity that Joseph is apparently not there when the magi come. The recipients of the gifts of these heroes from the East are 'the child, with Mary his mother' (2:11). So Mary is there, even if completely passive, at a very important moment in the unfolding of the narrative.

Luke

Luke is the principal New Testament source of material concerning Our Lady; and Luke has a supreme gift as a painter of pictures (it is almost certain that your favourite New Testament passage comes from Luke), which means that his material has seized the imagination of Christians all down the ages, and thrown down the gauntlet to a thousand artists.

Here are the relevant texts. First and foremost there is the Annunciation to Mary (1:26-38), possibly the story most frequently attempted by painters since the Gospels were first produced. It balances the preceding story, the Annunciation to Zechariah (1:5-23),[114] and the two episodes should be read together if possible. After that, Luke sweeps us straight into the next compelling episode, which should likewise be read with the other stories, the tale of Mary's visit to Elisabeth, often called the Visitation (1:39-46). Then comes the deeply subversive song that we call the Magnificat (1:46-56). underlining that Mary cannot be made unthinkingly to stand for the 'status quo'.

In the next chapter, we read of Mary giving birth in unpromising, even slightly shocking circumstances (2:1-7).[115] Still less promising, and decidedly shocking,

---

113. E. Anne Clements, *Mothers on the Margin: the Significance of the Women in Matthew's Genealogy* (Pickwick Publications, 2014).

114. Since Luke is such a gifted artist, it is important to read these episodes for the mood that they create rather than for any facts they may be said to report.

115. 'Unpromising' would describe the fact that Mary is compelled by a decree of the powers who run the world to make the journey from Galilee to Bethlehem, and that the child has to be put in a 'feeding-trough', because there is 'no room in the dwelling-place'; 'shocking' aptly covers Luke's mention, right at the end of the sentence, of Mary's pregnancy, even though she is only engaged.

is the cast of witnesses whom Luke assembles to hear what the angels have to say, and to be the first people to see the child Jesus. For these people are shepherds, who live on the margins of society, and are not even respectable enough to sleep at nights.

More important yet is what Luke tells us of Mary's reaction to these strange events: 'Mary was keeping all these things to herself, giving careful thought to them in her mind' (2:19). Luke repeats this idea, if not the precise wording, later in the same chapter (2:51, 'his mother was treasuring all these things in her heart'), so it is clearly important to him. I suggest that the best way to take it is as 'a rule for reading the gospel'. The reader is invited to imitate Mary's contemplative reading of the situation, so that all these beautifully told tales take us deeper into the mystery of who Jesus is, and of how we are to respond to him. Mary, that is to say, models the ideal human reaction to the mystery. The stories about Mary in the first two chapters of Luke are 'rules for reading the gospel'.

The next two episodes, Jesus' circumcision and naming, and his presentation in the Temple, tell us little of Mary beyond that she and her son were involved in Jewish Temple piety, and that Luke applauds them for this; and she is also obedient to what God (in the guise of the angel, see 1:31; 2:21), has told her to do. All this, then, is the story of God and the story of Jesus. Those two stories, of course, are now brought together in the final episode of Luke's infancy narrative, that extraordinary and poignant tale of Jesus' disappearance and rediscovery, precociously engaged in theological discussions 'in the midst of the teachers, and listening to them, and asking them questions'. Jesus is only doing what comes naturally to him,[116] but Luke enables us to hear the pain of Mary as she copes with his need to be 'on my Father's business', and redefining what it means to speak of family. This is presumably the first example of what Simeon had told her a few verses earlier, at the Presentation, that 'a sword of sorrow will pierce your heart' (2:35).

Oddly enough, Mary is not mentioned in Luke's version of the episode in the synagogue in Nazareth (4:16-30),[117] and, as we have seen, Luke (characteristically enough) gives a milder version of what we found in Mark 3:31-5,[118] and only a minor downplaying of Mary in response to the woman who speaks up, implicitly praising her (11:27, 28, where the woman says something like, 'Your mother must be very proud of you', and Jesus places a characteristic counter-emphasis on 'hearing the word of God and keeping it').

So, on the whole, Luke, who is the major source for New Testament stories about Mary, supports our general view that what is said about Mary has to be

---

116. 'Just like every lippy adolescent', as a Dominican friend once remarked to me.
117. Contrast Mark 6:3 and Matthew 13:55.
118. See Luke 8:19-21, where Jesus commends 'those who hear the will of God and do it'.

understood as being really about Jesus (and therefore about God) and about humanity at its very best. The only other passage where Luke mentions her is at Acts 1:14, the only time when Our Lady gets attention in the second volume, but, significantly enough, she is seen with the apostles and 'the women', joined in prayer ahead of the appointment of Matthias to the Twelve, and before Pentecost. This may give a flavour of how Luke sees her in the time after Jesus' death and resurrection.

John

Mary is mentioned only twice in John's Gospel, and on neither occasion is she named. Nevertheless, these two references are of immense importance, since they come at the beginning and the end, and both point to Mary's significance – namely, that she points to who Jesus is, and to how human beings are to respond.

The first is the remarkable story of the wedding feast at Cana (2:1-12), which for John constitutes the first of the 'signs' that tell the reader who Jesus really is. It is a very striking tale; it starts 'on the third day', which any Christian reader or hearer must have recognised as a reference to the Resurrection, but also completes a 'week' in which, if you count up the number of times the evangelist says 'on the next day' (1:29, 35, 43), we have gone deeper into the mystery of who Jesus is. Jesus' mother makes an implicit response to the lack of wine, and Jesus recognises it as such, but apparently rejects the request: 'What is that to you and me, woman? My hour has not yet come.' Nevertheless, she is not discouraged, and to our astonishment tells the attendants, 'Whatever he tells you, do.' The result is electrifying: 180 gallons of the very best wine, and the Master of Ceremonies tells the bridegroom that 'you have kept the good wine until now'.

Notice, however, how undramatic the story is: the 'miracle' is hardly described at all, simply mentioned as 'water-turned-into-wine'; and Jesus himself is almost at a distance from it. The important comment comes at the end, when the evangelist says, 'He did this as the beginning of his signs in Cana of the Galilee; and he revealed his glory. And his disciples came to faith in him.' Strikingly, his mother is not mentioned at this point, presumably because we are to understand that she did not need to come to faith in him, but points the message to us: 'Whatever he tells you, do.' There is also the implication, I take it, that the mother of Jesus is interested in the anxieties of ordinary people (though there was at one stage a fashion among biblical scholars disapproving of excess drinking of alcohol to try to downplay any idea that Jesus could go in for such an extravagant display!). This story, then, presents us with a Mary who points to the glory of her son, and away from herself, and also towards the meaning of human life.

The other occasion on which Mary appears in the fourth Gospel is at the foot of the cross (19:25-7). The fourth evangelist tells the story of Jesus' Passion in a very different way from the approach taken by Mark, for example, which is a bleak enough narrative. In John's version, Jesus is very much in charge, and here on the cross we are privileged witnesses to his founding a new dynasty, built on his mother and the Beloved Disciple. Here Mary neither does nor says anything, but silently points to the future, after the death, and after the Resurrection. Without a word or a gesture she indicates the mystery of Jesus' identity, and how human beings should respond. We watch with admiration as the Beloved Disciple 'took her to his own'.

Revelation

And that is almost it; but the last book of the entire Bible has something else to say. It is the vision of the sign of the Ark of the Covenant, the woman clothed with the sun (Revelation 11:19–12:18). It comes after the blowing of the seventh trumpet, when the reader (or audience) has a sense that the judgement on the world is coming to its climax, but that there is still trouble afoot. Not for the first time in this remarkable book, we are permitted a glimpse into the heavenly liturgy, which (if we read it aright) tells us what is actually going on in this rather alarming world of ours. The 'great sign' is that of a 'woman clothed with the sun, and the moon beneath her feet, and on her head a crown of 12 stars', symbolising the whole of God's creation. She is in her birth agony, threatened by the menace of the Dragon, which is waiting to 'devour her child when it is born'. The child is clearly Jesus, for it is 'going to shepherd all the nations with an iron rod', and is snatched up 'to God and to his throne', while the woman escapes to the desert, where she is rescued from the Dragon's attempts to destroy her.

Who is the woman? The most obvious reading, of course, is that she is the mother of Jesus, the subject of this chapter, who (we hope) can unite all Christians towards her son. In fairness, however, it is only proper to admit that she has also been understood (and not only in Protestant circles) as either Israel or the Church. I leave it to the reader to decide.

Two controversial doctrines

So, in the light of all this, what about the Catholic claim that Mary was 'conceived without original sin' and that she was 'assumed body and soul into heaven'? Are these two doctrines, of the Immaculate Conception, defined in 1854, and the Assumption (1951) simply inventions aimed at obscuring the pure light of the gospel and trapping the Catholic faithful in darkness? Or do they point either to the mystery of Jesus or the mystery of humanity?

The Immaculate Conception

Already in St Augustine you have the idea that 'the Lord conquered sin in her in every respect',[119] and it was, of course, Augustine who introduced into Western theology the notion of 'original sin'. Now over the centuries Christian thinkers grappled with this difficult idea, and in particular how to speak both of Mary's holiness, necessary if she was to be the Mother of God, and of her status as a creature. It did not come easily, but gradually there emerged the notion of Mary as a 'great exception' to the universal rule of being born in sin, while all were agreed that Mary was saved by Christ, who was himself the 'only exception'. The doctrine was commended by the Council of Basel in 1439, as a pious doctrine to be held and practised by all Catholics; but the Council of Trent, dealing with the crisis of the Reformation, had other things on its mind and stopped short of defining the doctrine. By the time that action was taken, by Pius IX in 1854, it was complicated and overshadowed by questions of whether the Pope, acting on his own, had authority to define a dogma for the whole Church. It was also, we may feel, bedevilled by nineteenth-century rationalism, both outside and within the Church.

What can we say about it today? There are three important ideas here: first, the humanity of Jesus, on which Christians are always a bit wobbly, but which Mary guarantees; second, the need for the Mother of God to be holy; third, the transfiguration of all humanity back into the divine likeness. The doctrine of the Immaculate Conception tries to hold all three of these ideas together without at any point surrendering the important insight that Mary, like us, needed to be saved by her son. It is not easy, but Christian thinkers have not invented it, or, for that matter, the doctrine of the Trinity, in order to baffle us, but in order to do justice to the instincts of ordinary Christians; Pelikan reflects that Marian doctrines are almost always 'imposed from below on the ecclesiastical authorities by what is in some sense a democratic process',[120] and that is a point which we should endeavour to keep in mind, possibly reinforcing it with memories of Christian artists who, long before 1854, found themselves painting the Immaculate Conception.

The Assumption

What are we to say about this more recently defined[121] doctrine? Like the Immaculate Conception, the definition of this dogma was rejected by both the Eastern Orthodox and the Reformed tradition; and it came at an unlucky time, when the churches were moving together, when Protestant theologians were becoming aware of the role of tradition in the formation of Scripture,

---

119. On Nature and Grace, 36. 42.
120. Pelikan, *Mary through the Ages*, p.186.
121. By Pius XII, not currently the most popular of pontiffs, admittedly, in 1950.

Catholic theologians were learning to insist more on the primacy of divine grace and the central role of what you might call 'justifying faith', and Protestants were wrestling with the importance of good works.[122] What this doctrine seeks to do is to express the effect upon humanity, with Mary as its archetypal representative, of what Jesus did, seen as 'victory over death'. But there is more to it than this, for Carl Jung, offspring of a long line of Swiss Protestants, argued that Catholic teachings about Mary offer a counter to the remoteness of God, softening it and making God more accessible.

There is a further point, which ought to be taken seriously, that it seems that no city ever claimed to possess Mary's bones, which is very unusual, and may say something about the circumstances of her death. Nor, it must be said, was there anything new about this doctrine; the Assumption has been celebrated on 15 August since at least the Middle Ages, and Mary's 'dormition' was frequently painted, often with the Apostles,[123] and with Enoch and Elijah, who were both 'taken up' (Genesis 5:24; 2 Kings 2:11, 12), in the understanding of the Old Testament authors.

What does the doctrine do? It has Mary represent the human race and the subtle relation in us between divine grace and human freedom, and offers an image of the gift given by God, of victory over sin and death, seen already in her.

Conclusion

Christians agree to call Mary 'blessed' in the words of the Magnificat (Luke 1:48), and we should perhaps listen, as Pope Francis is currently inviting us to do, to the insights of popular religion. It is worth asking why Mary has not lost her hold on the imagination of most Christians in a secular age; it is not because bishops have made dogmatic statements, but because Mary speaks to us today. It is not idle or sentimental to understand her as a mother who longs for her son's family to be reunited, and therefore to make her a patroness of the ecumenical movement.

---

122. In this section I have been very much influenced by the clarity and depth of Pelikan, *Mary Through the Ages*, pp. 203-205.
123. From Acts 1:13, 14.

Select Bibliography

Avis, P., 'Are we Receiving "Receptive Ecumenism"?', *Ecclesiology* 8 (2012), pp.223-34.

Brown, R.E., Donfried, K.P., Fitzmyer, J.A. and Reumann, J. (eds.), *Mary in the New Testament* (Paulist, 1978).

Clements, E.A., *Mothers on the Margin: the Significance of the Women in Matthew's Genealogy* (Pickwick Publications, 2014).

Dulles SJ, A., *The Reshaping of Catholicism: Current Challenges in the Theology of Church* (Harper and Row, 1988).

Hurley SJ, M., *Christian Unity: An Ecumenical Second Spring?* (Veritas, 1998).

John Paul II *Ut unum Sint* http://www.christlife.org/resources/articles/utunumsint.html

Küng, H. and Moltmann, J., eds, *Mary in the Churches* (Concilium, 1983).

Leeming SJ, B., *The Churches and the Church: A study of Ecumenism* (Darton, Longman and Todd, 1960).

Lohfink, G., *No Irrelevant Jesus: On Jesus and the Church Today* (Liturgical Press, 2014), chapter 9.

Murray, P., 'Introducing Receptive Ecumenism', *The Ecumenist* 51:2 (Spring 2014), pp.1-8.

O'Collins SJ, G., *On the Left Bank of the Tiber* (Gracewing, 2013) [chapters on John Paul II].

Paul VI *Ecclesiam Suam* http://www.vatican.va/holy_father/paul_vi/encyclicals/documents/hf_p-vi_enc_06081964_ecclesiam_en.html

Pelikan, J., *Mary through the Ages* (Yale University Press, 1998).

Pelikan, J., Flusser, D. and Lang, J., *Mary: Images of the Mother of Jesus in Jewish and Christian Perspective* (Fortress Press, 2005).

Rudd, D. in *Vatican II, Voice of the Church*, http://www.vatican2voice.org/6unity/restore_unity.htm

Sachs SJ, J.R., 'Catholicism in a New Key', in Colberg, K.M. and Krieg, R.A. (eds), *The Theology of Cardinal Walter Kasper* (Liturgical Press, 2014), pp.170-88.

Yarnold SJ, E., *They are in Earnest: Christian Unity in the Statements of Paul VI, John Paul I, John Paul II* (St Paul Publications, 1982).

Other books Nicholas has written for Kevin Mayhew

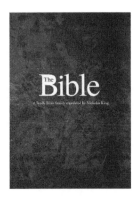

The Bible

A Study Bible freshly translated by Nicholas King

Available in various editions, please see our website for details.

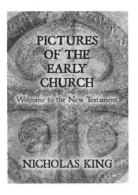

Pictures of the Early Church

Welcome to the New Testament

1501521

Please visit **www.kevinmayhew.com**
to discover more by Nicholas King